BUSINESS FORECASTING
ON YOUR
PERSONAL COMPUTER

BUSINESS FORECASTING ON YOUR PERSONAL COMPUTER

Neil Seitz

Reston Publishing Company, Inc.
A Prentice-Hall Company
Reston, Virginia

Library of Congress Cataloging in Publication Data

Seitz, Neil
    Business forecasting on your personal computer.

    Includes index.
    1. Business forecasting—Data processing. 2. Micro-
computers. I. Title.
HD30.27.S455 1984   338.5′442   83–23054
ISBN 0–8359–0607–8

Editorial/production supervision and interior design
by Norma M. Karlin

CONTENTS

v

Contents

PREFACE

Large organizations have long had access to powerful business forecasting methods through million-dollar computers, expensive program packages, and trained specialists. For people outside the structure who wanted to utilize the same methods, the only alternative was a costly one: subscribing to an expensive time-sharing system that frequently required extensive training.

With the advent of powerful, reasonably priced personal computers, the problem of prohibitive cost has been eliminated. Now millions of new users—families, small businesses, clubs—have access to these small marvels and to their manifold capabilities. Furthermore, many of those people having access to the large computer of their organization are opting for the convenience and ease of handling of the small machine.

While the problem of cost has been remedied, the problem of appropriate computer programs and instructions has not. The forecasting materials written for use on large computers are not only difficult to translate but are also unsuited for use on the personal computer. Consequently, this book was written to provide explanations and inexpensive programs—specifically business forecasting methods—for personal computer users.

This book contains explanations of a range of forecasting techniques sufficiently broad to deal with most forecasting problems; yet it is not necessary to learn all of them to begin forecasting. From the many forecasting methods available for each type of forecasting problem, a single method was selected for inclusion in this book. Each chosen method is one that has been widely used, can be easily learned, and can be used with a personal computer. BASIC language programs are included to make it possible to forecast without acquiring additional, expensive programs. Although the book and accompanying programs can be used on a large computer without difficulty, both were specifically designed for use on a simple personal computer.

BUSINESS FORECASTING
ON YOUR
PERSONAL COMPUTER

1

INTRODUCTION

Every business, government agency, nonprofit organization, and individual investor uses forecasts in making decisions. Decision makers can improve the quality of those forecasts by taking advantage of the availability and capabilities of inexpensive personal computers.

As almost all forecasts are based on the assumption that the item to be forecast is affected by something else, the first step in forecasting is to decide which factors are likely to affect the item being forecast. A businessman may believe that sales of his product are affected by overall economic conditions. Alternatively, he may believe that sales of his product simply grow over time; that is, the passage of time itself affects sales. The next step is to decide how to use those factors in preparing a forecast.

Forecasts may be either subjective or objective. A subjective forecast of stock prices can be prepared by reading extensively about the company and the economy, and then combining this information through some unspecified judgment process to come up with a forecast. The advantage of the subjective approach is that the forecaster can consider a mass of information; the disadvantage is that there is no systematic way to improve forecast accuracy by learning from past mistakes.

The objective approach involves developing a model which is generally constructed by studying past relationships between the item to be forecast and factors thought to affect it. The businessman

1

wishing to forecast sales could use an objective model based on the passage of time, economic conditions, or both.

Objective forecasting methods have several advantages over the subjective variety. Because they are objective, the forecasts are not affected by what the forecaster wishes the outcome to be. Many of the objective methods also include processes by which the forecasting model learns from its past errors. In addition, objective methods are frequently less time consuming than subjective approaches. Perhaps most importantly, objective methods provide a basis for evaluating forecast accuracy and for developing confidence ranges for forecasts.

A SURVEY OF FORECASTING PROBLEMS

Forecasting problems can be divided into three distinct types. The first type involves forecasting the *amount* of something, e.g., sales, accounts receivable, birth rates, or stock prices. The second type of forecast involves the *timing* of some event, such as the date on which a machine part will fail. The third type of forecast involves the *probability* of some events occurring. One might wish to know the probability of rain on July 15 of next year. The timing of a machine failure can be converted to an amount question by asking how many hours the machine will operate before failure. Many other timing forecasts can be converted to amount forecasts in a similar manner. Likewise, probability forecasts can frequently be turned into amount forecasts. Past rainfall patterns can be used to predict the number of days of rain next July, and the probability of rain on any one day can be based on the total number of rainy days expected.

This book concentrates on forecasts of amounts as they are the most common forecasting problems. Since many other problems can be restated as amount forecasts, the methods covered in this book are widely applicable.

Forecasts can also be classified according to the distance into the future the prediction is to cover. A sales forecast for inventory control purposes may cover only a few weeks while a sales forecast for a plant expansion decision may cover ten or twenty years. The methods discussed in this book have been used to prepare forecasts covering periods from several hours to several decades.

Forecasts can also be classified according to whether they are repetitive or one-time. A plant expansion decision will require one-time forecasts, or at least forecasts that are not going to be repeated on a regular basis. For inventory control, it may be necessary to prepare new forecasts for each of a thousand items every week. While it may be worthwhile to invest a substantial sum in a forecast for the plant expansion decision, the same investment in each of a thousand weekly inventory demand forecasts would be impossible. Methods for both repetitive and one-time forecasts are covered in this book.

Forecasts also differ with regard to the nature of the explanatory factors. If the forecaster feels that time is the only factor that needs to be considered, there are several very economical methods for examining the movement of a variable over time. These are widely used for short-term forecasting. Other methods in this book are available for the many occasions in which a factor or factors other than time are considered important.

Finally, forecasting methods differ with regard to computer hardware needed. All of the methods in this book have been used with only the aid of an inexpensive personal computer; many of them, with only a calculator.

A SURVEY OF FORECASTING METHODS

Numerous methods have been developed for dealing with the various types of forecasting problems cited above. The methods selected for inclusion in this book are widely recognized as easy to use and as sufficient to provide forecasting methods for a wide variety of problems.

Regression Analysis

Regression analysis is by far the most widely used method for forecasting the values of items that are affected by factors other than simply the passage of time. A technique for developing a model of the relationship between the item to be forecast and other factors (called explanatory variables) that are believed to affect it, regression analysis is most widely used for intermediate-term forecasts—those for periods of a few months to a few years.

Simple regression is used when the impact of only one explanatory variable is to be considered, for example, a study of hospital admissions using unemployment as the only explanatory variable. The main cost of simple regression is in collecting historical data on the item to be forecast and on the explanatory variables. Since many pocket calculators have built-in programs for simple regression, hardware needs are minimal. Because simple regression is so easy to use, it is possible to consider several factors that may affect the variable to be forecast before selecting the best variable to use.

Multiple regression is used when two or more factors affect the item to be forecast. It is a powerful tool and is widely used for intermediate-term forecasting. Some good calculators have built-in programs for problems involving two explanatory variables. Most personal computers have programs available for multiple regression with two or more explanatory variables. The main cost in using this method is the time required to collect historical data on the explanatory variables.

Nonlinear regression differs from the regression methods previously discussed in that it does not assume a linear relationship between the variable to be forecast and the explanatory variable. An example of a linear relationship is a formula explaining natural gas usage in a particular city, determined by studying the use of natural gas each day for six months:

$$\text{Usage} = 1{,}000 - 10 \cdot \text{temperature}$$

If this relationship were plotted on a graph, it would appear as in Figure 1-1(a). A nonlinear relationship would be of some other form, such as

$$\text{Usage} = 1{,}000/\text{temperature}$$

This relationship would appear as in Figure 1-1(b).

When simple or multiple regression has been attempted and it is discovered that the relationship is not a linear one, nonlinear regression is used.

Time Series Methods

Time series methods are used to forecast the value of an item by studying past movements of that item. For instance, one might forecast

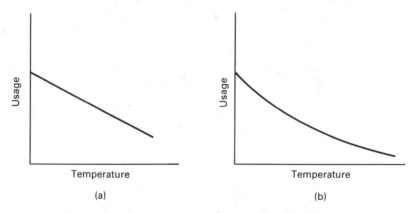

FIGURE 1-1 Gas Usage: Linear and Nonlinear Relationships

sales for the next week by studying the pattern in weekly sales over the past year. While time series forecasting is most widely used for short-term forecasts of up to a few months, it is sometimes possible to observe a very stable trend and to use it to forecast years into the future. Time series methods have the advantage of requiring as data only the historical values for the series itself. Since collection of data is frequently the most time consuming and expensive part of the forecasting project, these methods are generally economical to use.

Trend analysis involves the use of linear and nonlinear regression with time as the explanatory variable and is used when the item to be forecast displays some pattern over time. Population studies are a classic example of trend analysis. Although nonlinear regression can be completed using a calculator, it can be time consuming to test the various possible relationships. A personal computer is a major aid.

Decomposition analysis is used to identify several patterns that may appear simultaneously in a time series; e.g., monthly sales may reflect both long-term trends and seasonal variations. Because preparing a new decomposition analysis forecast is almost as time consuming as completing the first forecast, decomposition analysis is normally used when a forecast is required only once or infrequently.

In addition to its use in forecasting, decomposition analysis is used to *deseasonalize* a series. Often, the seasonal pattern must be removed from a series so that other factors which may be affecting it can be determined. Economic statistics released by the government frequently carry the notation that they have been *deseasonalized;* i.e., the seasonal pattern has been removed using a form of decomposition analysis.

Moving average analysis is another relatively simple procedure for examining a time series and preparing a forecast. The moving average approach forecasts future values based on some weighted average of past values. While moving average methods can be used with a seasonal pattern present, most are not well suited for this. Yet, they are easy to update, making them useful when repeated forecasts are needed and the series has no seasonal pattern. Most moving average approaches can be used with a simple calculator. However, *adaptive filtering,* a type of moving average analysis that includes a method for learning from past errors, requires a computer because of the many tedious calculations involved.

Exponential smoothing is actually a moving average form of time series forecasting, but the moving average is computed in a way that has the advantages of:

1. making it efficient to use with seasonal patterns present;
2. making it easy to adjust the forecasting model in response to past errors; and

3. making it very easy to prepare new forecasts once the first forecast has been prepared.

Thus, exponential smoothing is ideal for situations like inventory control, in which many forecasts must be prepared. Setting up the procedure for the first forecast is somewhat time consuming, but preparing new forecasts and updating the forecasting model is so simple that the method has been frequently used where the forecasts were to be updated manually.

Simulation Models

Like regression, simulation is used when the item to be forecast is affected by other variables. A simulation model describes some situation through a series of equations. The model provides a convenient basis for testing the impacts of various factors that might affect the item(s) to be forecast. Many firms have financial models which can be used to forecast profits or funds needs for various possible world circumstances. Models may be *certainty* models that give only the most likely outcome, or they may be *probability* models that give a range of possible outcomes for each set of events tested. Simulation models are substantially more time consuming to construct than are other forecasting methods discussed in this book. Knowledge of algebra and computer programming may be required. Probability models also require that you know the rules of probability. However, there are modeling packages such as VisiCalc® and SuperCalc™ that ease the job considerably.

SELECTION OF A FORECASTING METHOD

The three primary considerations in selecting a forecasting method are appropriateness, cost, and accuracy. An appropriate method not only fits the factors thought to affect the item to be forecast but also fits the forecasting situation; e.g., a technique appropriate for one-time forecasts would not be used for inventory control.

The questions of accuracy and cost involve a trade-off. It is possible to get a better forecast by spending more time and money, but it is necessary to decide if the extra accuracy is worth the extra cost. Although there are formulas for weighing the value of increased accuracy, it is difficult to know how much a particular method will increase forecast accuracy until it has been tried. Also, the benefit of increased accuracy is frequently decreased risk rather than decreased cost. Consequently, it is necessary to rely on judgment to determine how much effort to exert and, in turn, which forecasting method to use. Table 1-1 provides a summary of the features of each method to help in preliminary selection.

Table 1-1
OVERVIEW OF FORECASTING METHODS

Method	Ch.	Time Horizon*	Appropriate Use	Minimum Computing Hardware	Effort Required
Simple linear regression	2	Intermediate term	Item to be forecast is believed to be linearly related to one other variable.	Calculator	Collection of historical data for the two variables is normally the most time-consuming part of the forecast.
Multiple linear regression	3	Intermediate term	Item to be forecast is believed to be linearly related to more than one other variable.	Calculator for two variables. Computer for more than two.	Collection of historical data for all variables is the most time-consuming part of the forecast.
Nonlinear regression	4	Intermediate term	Item to be forecast is believed to be related to one or more other variables in a nonlinear way.	Calculator (Many have programs to examine nonlinear relationships but the process can be time consuming without a computer.)	Collection of historical data plus experimenting with several nonlinear models is required.

Table 1-1 (Continued)

Method	Ch.	Time Horizon*	Appropriate Use	Minimum Computing Hardware	Effort Required
Trend analysis	4	Intermediate to long term	Nonlinear simple regression when time is the variable to which the item we wish to forecast is related.	Calculator (Same comment as for nonlinear regression is applicable.)	Only requires the history of the item to be forecast, but experimenting with trend shapes takes time.
Decomposition	5	Short term	One-time short-term forecasts or elimination of seasonal components before using another forecasting method.	Calculator	Only history of the series is needed. Calculations are tedious unless a computer or good programmable calculator is available.
Moving averages	6	Short term	Repeated forecasts without seasonal patterns.	Calculator	Only requires history of the item to be forecast. Each forecast is quick, but original weight selection is time consuming.
Adaptive filtering	6	Short term	Repeated forecasts without seasonal patterns when the nature of any trend pattern may change over time.	Computer	Only requires history of the item to be forecast. Developing and checking model specifications can be time consuming.

Table 1-1 (Continued)

Method	Ch.	Time Horizon*	Appropriate Use	Minimum Computing Hardware	Effort Required
Exponential smoothing	7	Short term	Repeated forecasts with or without seasonal patterns.	Computer (Needed to set up the model. New forecasts could then be prepared easily with a calculator.)	Only requires history of the item to be forecast. Easiest method of all for repeated forecasts, but setting up the model takes as long as with adaptive filtering.
Simulation	8	Intermediate and long term	Repeated forecasts will be needed and accuracy or detail are worth a considerable investment of time.	Knowledge of a computer programming language or an electronic worksheet program.	Data collection and model construction take longer than for any of the above methods.

*Forecasters generally think of short term as under three months and intermediate term as three months to five years. Time horizons should be thought of as only general guidelines and are often ignored.

ORGANIZATION OF THE BOOK

It is not necessary to learn all of the forecasting methods in this book to begin forecasting. This book is organized according to forecasting methods, with each chapter devoted to one method. Table 1-1 and the brief description in Chapter 1 can be used to identify the forecasting method that is likely to fit a particular problem. The reader can then turn to the chapter on that method without studying the chapters covering other methods.

In Chapter 8, two approaches to modeling and simulation are discussed: one requiring the use of an electronic worksheet program such as VisiCalc® or SuperCalc™ and the other requiring knowledge of computer programming. Because Chapter 8 is geared toward only those readers meeting the requirements, it can be passed over with no loss in understanding other than with regard to these particular techniques—modeling and simulation.

The statistical terms that are used in this book can be found in Appendix A. Although the use of these forecasting methods does not require mathematical ability above elementary high school algebra, a review of the terms is recommended before continuing. In addition, you should review Chapters 9 and 10 before beginning a forecasting project. Chapter 9 contains special information on collecting and managing data; Chapter 10, on evaluating forecast accuracy. Beyond this, the methods stand relatively independent of each other, making it possible to develop proficiency in only the method or methods appropriate for a specific problem.

2

SIMPLE
REGRESSION ANALYSIS

Most forecasting methods are based on the belief that the item to be forecast is related to something else. Just as a drink vendor at a sports stadium knows that drink sales are affected by temperature, an automobile dealer knows that car sales are affected by the price of gasoline and the unemployment rate, and a hospital administrator has a list of six or eight major factors that affect the number of patients in the hospital on a given day.

Regression analysis is the most widely used tool for formally analyzing such relationships and using those relationships to forecast. This chapter covers simple regression, the procedure used when the forecaster wishes to consider only one factor believed to affect the item to be forecast. Chapter 3 covers multiple regression, an expansion from simple regression to the simultaneous consideration of two or more factors that may be related to the item to be forecast.

THE REGRESSION MODEL

A drink vendor at a sports stadium will be used to illustrate the regression model. The vendor wishes to forecast drink sales and believes that temperature is the primary factor affecting sales. In regression terminology, drink sales are called the *dependent variable* and temperature is called the *independent variable.*

The vendor decides to study the relationship by putting the information on a graph (see Figure 2-1). Each dot represents the temperature on a particular day and the corresponding drink sales for that day. The line in the graph was drawn to fit the dots as closely as possible. The vendor can use this line to forecast. Suppose tomorrow's temperature will be 30°. The vendor can use Figure 2-1 to find that the expected sales level is about 400 cases.

The observations (dots) tend to lie near the line rather than precisely on it, indicating that temperature is not a perfect predictor of drink sales. Drink sales may vary for different reasons. An extremely close game, for example, will keep people's attention on the field rather than on their thirst. Suppose, then, the vendor observes that 90 percent of the time, drink sales do not exceed by more than 60 cases the amount predicted by the line on the graph. If he wants to have a 0.90 probability of not running out of drinks, he will need the expected 400 cases for a 30° temperature plus 60 extra cases—his margin of error.[1]

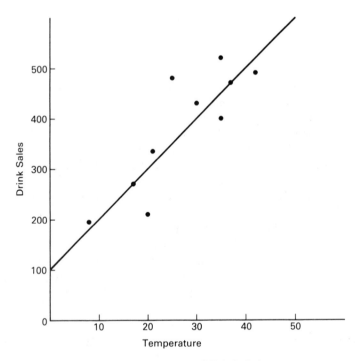

FIGURE 2-1 Graphical Analysis of Drink Sales

[1]The observant reader may note that tomorrow's temperature is not known and is, in fact, another forecast. The vendor may need to study the weather bureau's prediction and build in a margin for the weather bureau's errors as well.

Regression analysis achieves essentially the same thing that the vendor achieved with the graph: It establishes a line, called the regression line, and a measure of the margin for error. The difference is that regression does this in a precise, objective manner.

To develop the regression model, look again at the line drawn in Figure 2-1. Note that expected drink sales are 100 cases at a temperature of 0° and 400 cases at a temperature of 30°. Thus, the change in expected drink sales per degree increase in temperature is

$$\frac{400 - 100}{30 - 0} = 10$$

This relationship between drink sales and temperature can be stated as a mathematical equation:

$$\text{Drink sales} = 100 + 10 \cdot \text{temperature}$$

In standard regression analysis terminology, this line is expressed as

$$Y = a + bX \qquad\qquad (2\text{-}1)$$

where

Y = the dependent variable, or the variable to be forecast;

X = the independent variable, which is related to the item to be forecast;

a = the expected value of Y if X is zero; and

b = the expected change in Y for each unit change in X.

For the drink problem, Y is the level of drink sales, a is 100, b is 10, and X is the temperature.

The Least Squares Line

In the above example, a line was fitted to temperature and drink sales by simply drawing the line that looked best. The vendor probably tried to minimize the average deviation—the average distance from the dots to the line. Regression analysis uses a formula that fits a line so as to minimize the average squared deviation from the line. The approach tends to avoid larger errors because the squaring of deviations from the line results in placing more emphasis on minimizing large deviations.

The Regression Computation

Some calculators have built-in regression programs, and many computer programs for regression analysis are available; one such program appears at the end of this chapter. Consequently, it is only necessary to enter the X and Y values into a computer or calculator along with a few other instructions. However, it is still helpful to know how the computations are done. The basic formulas are

$$b = \sigma_{XY}/\sigma_X^2 \text{ and} \qquad (2\text{-}2)$$

$$a = \overline{Y} - b\overline{X} \qquad (2\text{-}3)$$

where

σ_{XY} = the covariance between X and Y;[2]

σ_X^2 = the variance of X;

$\overline{X}$ = the average value of X; and

$\overline{Y}$ = the average value of Y.

Table 2–1 contains drink sales and temperature observations in columns 2 and 3. The average value of column 4 is the covariance, and the average value of column 5 is the variance of X (temperature). The numbers in columns 6 through 8 will be used later in this chapter. The values of a and b are then

$$b = 985.5/101.2 = 9.74$$

$$a = 380 - 9.74 \cdot 27 = 117$$

Note that these numbers differ somewhat from the a and b estimates made when the line was fitted by eye. The difference results from the greater accuracy of the regression method and from the relatively greater emphasis the regression method places on reducing large deviations.

The regression model can now be used to forecast. If the temperature for tomorrow's game is 35°, expected drink sales are

$$\text{Expected sales} = 117 + 9.74 \cdot 35 = 458$$

Goodness of Fit

In the graphic example, the vendor looked at the graph and observed that sales seldom exceeded the line by more than 60 cases. He used this

[2] These terms are all explained in Appendix A.

Table 2-1
SAMPLE REGRESSION ANALYSIS: DRINK SALES

1 Period	2 Sales	3 Temperature	4 $(X-\overline{X})(Y-\overline{Y})$	5 $(X-\overline{X})^2$	6 $(Y-\overline{Y})^2$	7 $\hat{Y}$	8 $(Y-\hat{Y})^2$
1	430	30	150	9	2,500	409	441
2	335	21	270	36	2,025	322	169
3	520	35	1,120	64	19,600	458	3,844
4	490	42	1,650	225	12,100	526	1,296
5	470	37	900	100	8,100	477	49
6	210	20	1,190	49	28,900	312	10,404
7	195	8	3,515	361	34,225	195	0
8	270	17	1,100	100	12,100	283	169
9	400	35	160	64	400	458	3,364
10	480	25	−200	4	10,000	361	14,161
Sum	3,800	270	9,855	1,012	129,950		33,897
Average Sum/n	380	27	985.5	101.2	12,995		
Symbol of Average	$\overline{Y}$	$\overline{X}$	σ_{XY}	σ_X^2	σ_X^2		

information as a confidence range for the forecast. Regression analysis makes it possible to be more precise about confidence ranges. Estimates of confidence ranges are based on the goodness-of-fit measures in this section.

Standard Error

Recall that the regression line is the line that minimizes the average squared deviation. The standard error is the average squared error, or the average squared difference between the regression line and value of the dependent variable. The formula for the standard error (SE) is[3]

$$SE = \sqrt{\frac{\Sigma(Y-\hat{Y})^2}{n}} \tag{2-4}$$

[3] Many computer programs give the *standard error of the estimate* rather than the standard error. The standard error of the estimate for a simple regression problem is

$$\sqrt{[\Sigma(Y-\hat{Y})^2]/(n-2)}$$

where

$\hat{Y}$ = the expected value of Y for a particular value of X;

Y = the value of Y that actually occurred with that value of X; and

n = the number of observations.

The expected value of Y for each observed value of X appears in column 7 of Table 2-1. The square of the difference between the expected and actual value of Y appears in column 8. The standard error is found by summing column 8, dividing by n, and taking the square root of this result:[4]

$$SE = \sqrt{33,897/10} = 58$$

Coefficient of Determination

The coefficient of determination is an index of how close the relationship is between the dependent and independent variables. The coefficient has a value between zero and one, depending on the percent of variance in Y explained by the regression model. A formula for the coefficient of determination (r^2) is[5]

$$r^2 = 1 - \frac{SE^2}{\sigma_Y^2} \qquad (2\text{-}5)$$

Thus, the coefficient of determination is one minus the ratio of variance around the regression line—unexplained variance—to the total variance of Y.

---

[4] Some calculators and computer programs provide the correlation coefficient, but not the standard error. Fortunately, the standard error can be computed from the correlation coefficient:

$$SE = \sqrt{(1-r^2)\sigma_Y^2}$$

For the above problem, this yields a standard error of

$$SE = \sqrt{(1-0.74) \cdot 12,995} = 58$$

[5] In practice, a more convenient formula which yields exactly the same coefficient of determination is

$$r^2 = \left[\frac{\sigma_{XY}}{\sigma_X \sigma_Y} \right]^2$$

Using this formula and the information from Table 2-1, the coefficient of determination for the drink problem is

$$r^2 = 1 - \frac{58^2}{12,995} = 0.74$$

In other words, temperature changes accounted for 74 percent of the variation in drink sales.

A high r^2 means that the model does a good job of explaining movements in Y. The r^2 is frequently used to compare models, with the model having the highest r^2 being used.

Correlation Coefficient

The correlation coefficient is another widely used measure of goodness of fit. The formula for its computation is

$$r = \frac{\sigma_{XY}}{\sigma_X \sigma_Y} \qquad (2\text{-}6)$$

The correlation coefficient for drink sales is thus

$$r = \frac{985.5}{\sqrt{101.2} \; \sqrt{12,995}} = 0.86$$

Although the coefficient of determination is simply the square of the correlation coefficient, the two measures provide complementary information. Unlike the coefficient of determination, the correlation coefficient can be either positive or negative. A positive correlation coefficient means that the dependent variable tends to increase when the independent variable increases and tends to decrease when the independent variable decreases. Hence, the line in Figure 2-1 goes uphill from left to right indicating a positive correlation coefficient. A negative correlation coefficient would occur if the line sloped downhill from left to right. Although values of the correlation coefficient do not have a meaning as direct as the meaning of the coefficient of determination, similar interpretations are possible. The closer the correlation coefficient is to a plus or a minus one, the better is the fit between the dependent and independent variable.

Confidence Ranges

Suppose that one wants to choose a confidence range such that there is a 0.90 probability that any particular value of Y will fall within that range from $\hat{Y}$. A widely used formula for computing the approximate confidence range is[6]

$$\text{Confidence range} = \hat{Y} \pm t_{0.10} \text{ SE} \sqrt{n/(n-2)} \qquad (2\text{-}7)$$

where $t_{0.10}$ is the value from the table of the t statistic (Appendix A) for eight degrees of freedom and 0.10 probability of the value falling outside the range.[7] The approximate confidence range for drinks is then

$$\hat{Y} \pm 1.860 \cdot 58 \sqrt{10/8} = \hat{Y} \pm 121$$

Thus, the vendor can say that there is approximately a 0.90 probability of drink sales falling within $\pm$ 121 of the regression line. For a temperature of 35°, there is a 0.90 probability that drink sales will be between 337 and 579. The confidence range for any other probability can be determined by using another column of the t statistic table.

The t statistic for eight degrees of freedom was used because the appropriate t statistic value for a simple regression is the one for degrees of freedom equal to two less than the number of observations.

Although the approximate confidence interval in equation 2-7 is widely used in practice, a more precise measurement of the confidence interval is

$$\hat{Y} \pm t_{0.10} \text{ SE} \sqrt{n/(n-2)} \sqrt{1 + \frac{1}{n} + \frac{(X_o - \overline{X})^2}{n\sigma_X^2}} \qquad (2\text{-}8)$$

where X_o is the value of X for which one wishes to predict Y. For a temperature of 35°, the more precise 0.90 confidence interval is

$$458 \pm 1.860 \cdot 58 \sqrt{10/8} \sqrt{1 + \frac{1}{10} + \frac{(35-27)^2}{10 \cdot 101.2}} = 458 \pm 130$$

[6] If you are using a computer program that gives the standard error of the estimate (see note 3), formula 2-7 reduces to

$$\text{Confidence range} = \hat{Y} \pm t_{10} \text{ standard error of the estimate}$$

[7] The two-tailed probability column is used because the question is simply whether sales will fall outside of a particular range in either direction. The one-tailed probability would be used, for example, if one wanted to know the sales level that there was a 0.10 probability of exceeding.

USING REGRESSION ANALYSIS
TO FORECAST

Of course, the end product of the regression analysis must be the preparation of a forecast. There are several things to consider before using regression analysis to forecast.

First, there is the question of the availability of data. History is needed for both the dependent and independent variables. While the example in this chapter used ten observations on each variable, this is a small number of observations. An examination of the table of values of the *t* statistic shows that the confidence interval for a forecast becomes smaller as the number of observations increases. For the drink sales example, the 0.90 confidence interval was ±121. If the number of observations were increased from ten to thirty, the degrees of freedom would increase from eight to twenty-eight, and the 0.90 confidence range would decrease from ±121 to ±107.

In addition to historical data, one needs an estimate of X for the forecast period. Knowing that the value of steel producers' common stocks tends to go up and down with automobile manufacturers' common stocks is likely to be of little help in forecasting the price of a steel producer's common stock at the end of next month. Since we do not know whether the auto manufacturers' common stocks will rise or fall in price next month, the forecasting problem has simply been transferred. Recall that the confidence interval was for a given value of X. If the X for the forecast period is an estimate, the confidence interval increases.

Problems also arise if one forecasts far outside the range of values of X used in developing the regression model. Suppose an unseasonably warm 90° day occurs at the sports stadium. Because no observation was made above 42°, one really has little idea of what will happen in the range of 90°. For example, people may go to the beach instead of the sports stadium, resulting in a decline in sales rather than in an increase.

The passage of time also leads to difficulties. The relationship that existed last year may not hold several years in the future. If the drink vendor wished to extend the forecast several years into the future, he may need to consider the effects of winning and losing teams, economic conditions, etc. Consequently, the regression model should periodically be retested to be sure that past relationships still hold. In addition, judgment about the stability of relationships is required as the time horizon to which one is forecasting gets longer. Monitoring the accuracy of a forecasting method is discussed in more detail in Chapter 10.

Seasonality of data is another factor that can distort regression results. Suppose monthly automobile sales are used in a forecasting

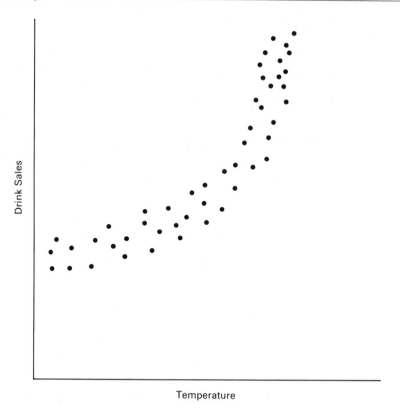

FIGURE 2-2 Example of a Nonlinear Relationship

model as a measure of consumer willingness to purchase capital goods. Results might be biased by the fact that automobile sales during certain months are affected by factors such as new model introduction and weather. To achieve accurate results, these seasonal factors should be removed from the series before the regression analysis is performed. Methods of removing seasonal patterns from data are discussed in Chapter 5.

Nonlinearity is another problem of regression analysis. The regression model is based on the fitting of a straight line to past observations. Suppose, however, the relationship between drink sales and temperature appeared as in Figure 2-2. A straight line fitted so that data will cause the model to underestimate sales in exceptionally warm weather and in exceptionally cold weather. Nonlinearity can frequently be discovered by visual examination of a graph such as Figure 2-2. If the relationship is nonlinear, procedures for nonlinear analysis can be used. These are explained in Chapter 4.

Autocorrelation is a problem that can occur for any number of reasons, including seasonality and nonlinearity. Autocorrelation exists if the error terms $(Y - \hat{Y})$ display any pattern over time. If an autocorrelation problem exists, an overestimate by the regression model in one period is likely to be followed by an overestimate in the following period, or an underestimate followed by another underestimate. The Durbin-Watson statistic (DW) gives an indication of autocorrelation:

$$DW = \frac{\displaystyle\sum_{t=2}^{n} (e_t - e_{t-1})^2}{\displaystyle\sum_{t=1}^{n} e_t^2}$$

where $e_t = (Y_t - \hat{Y}_t)$. The Durbin-Watson statistic for soft drink sales is computed in Table 2-2, using Y and $\hat{Y}$ data from Table 2-1.

As a rule of thumb, a Durbin-Watson statistic between 1.5 and 2.5 indicates no significant autocorrelation problem. Thus, the 1.94 Durbin-Watson statistic for drink sales leads to the conclusion that there is not an autocorrelation problem.

Autocorrelation problems can frequently be eliminated by restating the model in terms of change rather than total value. For

Table 2-2
DURBIN-WATSON STATISTIC COMPUTATIONS

t	Y_t	$\hat{Y}_t$	$Y_t - \hat{Y}_t$	$[(Y_t - \hat{Y}_t) - (Y_{t-1} - \hat{Y}_{t-1})]^2$	$(Y_t - \hat{Y}_t)^2$
1	430	409	21		441
2	335	322	13	64	169
3	520	458	62	2,401	3,844
4	490	526	−36	9,604	1,296
5	470	477	−7	841	49
6	210	312	−102	9,025	10,404
7	195	195	0	10,404	0
8	270	283	−13	169	169
9	400	458	−58	2,025	3,364
10	480	361	119	31,329	14,161
Sum				65,862	33,897

$$DW = \frac{65,862}{33,897} = 1.94$$

example, one could do a new regression analysis of drink sales using the following variables:

y = change in drink sales from the previous week, and

x = change in temperature from the previous week.

If autocorrelation still exists after this adjustment, it may be necessary to adjust for seasonal patterns using the methods discussed in Chapter 5 or to try nonlinear regression, discussed in Chapter 4.

A final factor related to time is particularly important when regression is used for forecasting. Sometimes a forecaster thinks he has developed a good forecasting model when, in fact, the independent variable is only a surrogate for the passage of time. For example, a model relating the number of heart surgeries to gross national product over a number of years may yield a relatively high correlation coefficient. However, this apparent relationship may result from the fact that both heart surgeries and GNP have increased over time rather than from any relationship between GNP and heart surgeries. A more accurate forecast might be had by simply using this month's actual heart surgeries—possibly with an adjustment for seasonal factors—as the forecast for next month. It is always worthwhile to check any forecasting model against a naive forecasting method of assuming that the outcome for next period will be the same as that for last period. Evaluation of relative accuracy is discussed in more detail in Chapter 10.

The above discussion of possible problems should not be misconstrued as detracting from the usefulness of regression analysis any more than notes on safe driving should be interpreted as detracting from the usefulness of an automobile. When used properly, the regression model is an extremely powerful forecasting tool.

RELATED TECHNIQUES

Two techniques closely related to simple regression are *multiple regression* and *nonlinear regression*. Each of these techniques is discussed in separate chapters. *Discriminant analysis* is closely related to regression analysis and is used when the dependent variable is stated as yes or no. Thus, it is used as a model much like regression to forecast the occurrence or nonoccurrence of events. For a discussion of discriminant analysis, see

Klecka, William R. *Discriminant Analysis.* Beverly Hills: Sage Publishing Company, 1982.

PROBLEMS

1. Shown below are stock prices, represented by the Standard and Poor's 500 Stock Index, and interest rates represented by the interest rates on long-term U.S. Government bonds. The data is on a quarterly basis with the first period being the first quarter of 1976 and the last period being the fourth quarter of 1981.

Period	Stock Prices	Interest Rates	Period	Stock Prices	Interest Rates
1	102.77	7.98%	13	101.59	8.98%
2	104.28	7.97	14	102.91	9.01
3	105.24	7.92	15	109.32	8.96
4	107.46	7.59	16	107.94	10.12
5	98.42	7.65	17	102.09	11.69
6	100.48	7.64	18	114.24	10.10
7	96.53	7.62	19	125.46	10.80
8	95.10	7.82	20	135.76	12.01
9	89.21	8.19	21	136.00	12.34
10	95.53	8.42	22	131.21	13.04
11	102.54	8.50	23	116.18	13.90
12	96.11	8.73	24	122.55	13.54

Perform a simple regression analysis on these data. Do you detect any problems with the regression model?

2. Convert the data in problem 1 from actual values to change from the previous period and perform a simple regression analysis on these changes. How do you explain the differences between this result and the result obtained in problem 1 with regard to the impact of interest rates on stock prices. If you wished to forecast stock prices based on expected interest rates, would you use the model developed in problem 1 or the model based on period-to-period change?

3. The interest rate for period 25 is expected to be 13 percent. Prepare a stock-price forecast and a 95 percent confidence interval for period 25.

4. Shown below are department store sales and disposable personal income for 1957 through 1981.

Year	Department Store Sales ($ billions)	Disposable Personal Income ($ billions)	Year	Department Store Sales ($ billions)	Disposable Personal Income ($ billions)
1957	12.0	308	1970	37.3	691
1958	12.6	317	1971	42.0	746
1959	13.6	337	1972	46.6	803
1960	13.9	349	1973	52.3	904
1961	14.5	364	1974	55.9	998
1962	15.8	384	1975	61.8	1,096
1963	18.5	402	1976	68.2	1,194
1964	20.8	438	1977	76.5	1,314
1965	23.4	472	1978	84.5	1,474
1966	26.1	508	1979	90.0	1,650
1967	29.6	547	1980	94.7	1,824
1968	33.3	590	1981	103.6	2,029
1969	36.4	634			

Perform a simple regression analysis on these data.

5. Disposable personal income for 1982 was $2,172.5 billion. Use the regression model developed in problem 4 to predict department store sales and a 95 percent confidence interval for 1982.

SIMPLE REGRESSION PROGRAM

This program performs simple linear regression, is short, and uses only the simplest BASIC language commands. Consequently, it can be used without modification on most personal computers. Despite its simplicity, the program provides all the information needed for simple regression forecasting.

The program contains a set of sample DATA statements to perform simple regression on the data in Table 2-1. To use the program, simply replace this data with your own. The first piece of data must be the number of observations. The second data set consists of all observations of the dependent variable. The third and final data set consists of all observations of the independent variable. The observations must be entered in order so that they can be correctly paired. For example, it is assumed that the third observation of the dependent variable was made in association with the third observation of the independent variable.

24

```
10  DIM A(120)
20  READ N
30  FOR I = 1 TO N
40  READ A(I)
50  NEXT I
60  FOR I = 1 TO N
70  READ A(N+I)
80  LET M = M + A(N+I)*A(N+I)
90  LET P = P + A(N+I)
100 LET Q = Q + A(I)
110 LET R = R + A(I)*A(N+I)
120 LET S = S + A(I)*A(I)
130 NEXT I
140 LET B = (N*R - P*Q)/(N*M - P*P)
150 LET C = Q/N - B*P/N
160 FOR I = 1 TO N
170 LET A(I) = A(I) - C - B*A(N+I)
180 IF I = 1 THEN 200
190 LET D = D + (A(I) - A(I-1))*(A(I) - A(I-1))
200 T = T + A(I)*A(I)
210 NEXT I
220 PRINT "A = ";C
230 PRINT "B = ";B
240 PRINT "COEF. OF DETERMINATION = ";(1 - T/(S - Q*Q/N))
250 PRINT "STANDARD ERROR = ";SQR(T/N)
260 PRINT "DURBIN-WATSON = ";(D/T)
270 PRINT
280 PRINT "TO FORECAST, ENTER A VALUE OF X (0=STOP)"
290 INPUT X
300 IF X=0 THEN 999
320 PRINT "THE PREDICTED VALUE OF Y IS ";C+B*X
330 GOTO 270
800 DATA 10
810 DATA 430,335,520,490,470
820 DATA 210,195,270,400,480
830 DATA 30,21,35,42,37,20,8,17,35,25
999 END
```

Usage

Some users will prefer to store data in separate files rather than in data statements. This can be done by simply eliminating the DATA statements and changing the READ statement according to your particular computer's file reading rules.

With most systems, this is accomplished by replacing READ with INPUT and a file name.

To enter the data from the terminal during operation, remove the DATA statements and replace statements 20 through 70 with the following

```
20  PRINT  "ENTER  THE  NUMBER  OF  OBSERVATIONS"
24  INPUT  N
27  PRINT  "ENTER  THE  DEPENDENT  VARIABLE,"
28  PRINT  "     ONE  OBSERVATION  PER  LINE"
30  FOR  I  =  1  TO  N
40  INPUT  A(I)
50  NEXT  I
55  PRINT  "ENTER  THE  INDEPENDENT  VARIABLE"
56  PRINT  "     ONE  OBSERVATION  PER  LINE"
60  FOR  I  =  1  TO  N
70  INPUT  A(N+I)
```

The first statement of the program—10 DIM A(120)—establishes space for the regression analysis. The number in parentheses must be at least twice the number of observations. The number 120 limits the program to 60 observations each for the dependent and independent variables. If you want to use more than 60 pairs of observations in the regression analysis, replace 120 with a number at least twice the number of observation pairs.

3

MULTIPLE REGRESSION

Simple linear regression involved one independent variable which was related to the item to be forecast. Multiple regression involves two or more independent variables. In the previous chapter, a drink vendor used the temperature to forecast soft drink sales at a sports stadium. The model was

$$\text{Drink sales} = a + b \cdot \text{temperature}$$

Based on historical data, regression analysis was used to estimate the regression coefficients: $a = 117$ and $b = 9.74$.

Suppose the vendor also knew that people drank more when the game was one-sided because they had time to concentrate on thirst rather than on the playing field. He might then decide to use the point spread at the end of the game as a second independent variable. The model would become

$$\text{Drink sales} = a + b \cdot \text{temperature} + c \cdot \text{spread}$$

There is no real limit to the number of variables that can be included in this manner. Frequently, using more than one independent variable results in substantial improvements in forecasting accuracy.

Although a few calculators have programs for two independent variables, a computer is generally used. For more than two independent variables, a computer is almost a necessity. In this chapter, the use of multiple regression is first illustrated for two independent variables. The regression model is then generalized to three or more independent variables.

TWO INDEPENDENT VARIABLES

As with simple regression, the formulas used in multiple regression will minimize the average squared difference between the observed and predicted values of the independent variable. The two-variable linear regression model is of the form:

$$Y = a + bX + cZ \qquad (3\text{-}1)$$

Y is the independent variable, a, b, and c are the regression coefficients, and X and Z are the independent variables. The formulas for the coefficients are

$$b = \frac{\sigma_{ZY}\sigma_{XZ} - \sigma_{XY}\sigma_Z^2}{(\sigma_{XZ})^2 - \sigma_X^2\sigma_Z^2} \qquad (3\text{-}2)$$

$$c = \frac{\sigma_{XY}\sigma_{XZ} - \sigma_{ZY}\sigma_X^2}{(\sigma_{XZ})^2 - \sigma_X^2\sigma_Z^2} \qquad (3\text{-}3)$$

$$a = \overline{Y} - b\overline{X} - c\overline{Z} \qquad (3\text{-}4)$$

As before, σ_{XY} is covariance between X and Y, as described in Appendix A. The other symbols also represent covariance and standard deviation as indicated.

Table 3–1 contains drink sales, temperature, and end-of-game point spread for ten games. Columns 5 through 10 provide the necessary summations for completing the regression model. Using these numbers, the coefficients for the drink problem are

$$b = \frac{354.5 \cdot 7.1 - 985.5 \cdot 30.2}{7.1^2 - 101.2 \cdot 30.2} = 9.0641$$

$$c = \frac{985.5 \cdot 7.1 - 354.5 \cdot 101.2}{7.1^2 - 101.2 \cdot 30.2} = 9.6074$$

$$a = 380 - 9.0641 \cdot 27 - 9.6074 \cdot 10 = 39.1953$$

A temperature of 35° is expected for tomorrow's game, and sportscasters predict an eight-point spread. The drink sales forecast for the game is therefore

Table 3-1
COMPUTATIONS FOR REGRESSION ANALYSIS: DRINK SALES

1 Period t	2 Sales Y	3 Temperature X	4 Spread Z	5 $(Y-\bar{Y})^2$	6 $(X-\bar{X})^2$	7 $(Z-\bar{Z})^2$	8 $(Y-\bar{Y})(X-\bar{X})$	9 $(Y-\bar{Y})(Z-\bar{Z})$	10 $(X-\bar{X})(Z-\bar{Z})$
1	430	30	12	2,500	9	4	150	100	6
2	335	21	10	2,025	36	0	270	0	0
3	520	35	22	19,600	64	144	1,120	1,680	96
4	490	42	6	12,100	225	16	1,650	−440	−60
5	470	37	8	8,100	100	4	900	−180	−20
6	210	20	2	28,900	49	64	1,190	1,360	56
7	195	8	9	34,225	361	1	3,515	185	19
8	270	17	8	12,100	100	4	1,100	220	20
9	400	35	6	400	64	16	160	−80	−32
10	480	25	17	10,000	4	49	−200	700	−14
Sum	3,800	270	100	129,950	1,012	302	9,855	3,545	71
Sum/n	380	27	10	12,995	101.2	30.2	985.5	354.5	7.1
Meaning	$\bar{Y}$	$\bar{X}$	$\bar{Z}$	σ_Y^2	σ_X^2	σ_Z^2	σ_{XY}	σ_{ZY}	σ_{XZ}

$$Y = 39.1953 + 9.0641 \cdot 35 + 9.6074 \cdot 8 = 433$$

Note that the b value for temperature is not the same as that determined using simple regression on the same data in Chapter 2. The multiple regression model considers joint impacts of the independent variables on the dependent variable. Thus, it is *not* possible to build a multiple regression model through a series of simple regression computations.

Goodness of Fit and Confidence Ranges

The measures of model accuracy that were used for simple regression generally apply for multiple regression as well.

Standard Error

As with simple regression, the standard error is a measure of the differences between values of Y and those values predicted by the model. It forms the basis for confidence interval estimates and other goodness-of-fit measures. The formula is the same as that for simple regression:[1]

$$SE = \sqrt{\Sigma(Y - \hat{Y})^2/n} \qquad (3\text{-}5)$$

where n equals the number of observations—ten in this case. Using the information from Table 3-2, the standard error is thus

$$SE = \sqrt{6,612/10} = 26$$

This compares to a standard error of 58 that was achieved with simple regression; multiple regression reduced the standard error by more than half. The benefits of this reduction show up in greater forecasting accuracy.

---

[1] An alternate formula that gives the same answer and is frequently easier to use in practice is

$$SE = \sqrt{(1+R^2)\sigma_Y^2}$$

where R^2 is the coefficient of determination, described on page 31. Using the previously determined r^2 of 0.948 from Table 3-2, the standard error is computed to be

$$SE = \sqrt{(1 - 0.948)12,995} = 26$$

Table 3-2
GOODNESS OF FIT AND DURBIN-WATSON TEST

1	2	3	4	5	6	7	8	9
Period	Sales	Temp.	Spread			$Y-\hat{Y}$	$(Y-\hat{Y})^2$	
t	Y	X	Z	$(Y-\overline{Y})^2$	$\hat{Y}$	e_t	e_t^2	$(e_t-e_{t-1})^2$
1	430	30	12	2,500	426	4	16	
2	335	21	10	2,025	326	9	81	25
3	520	35	22	19,600	568	−48	2,304	3,249
4	490	42	6	12,100	478	12	144	3,600
5	470	37	8	8,100	451	19	361	49
6	210	20	2	28,900	240	−30	900	2,401
7	195	8	9	34,225	198	−3	9	729
8	270	17	8	12,100	270	0	0	9
9	400	35	6	400	414	−14	196	196
10	480	25	17	10,000	429	51	2,601	4,225
Sum	3,800			129,950			6,612	14,483
Sum/n	380			12,995				

Coefficient of Determination

The multiple coefficient of determination (R^2) measures the percent of variance of Y around its mean that is explained by the regression model. The formula is the same as for the simple coefficient of determination discussed in Chapter 2:

$$R^2 = 1 - \frac{SE^2}{\sigma_Y^2} \qquad (3\text{-}6)$$

As with simple regression, $R^2 = 0$ means the regression model explained none of the movement of Y while $R^2 = 1.0$ means that the model explained all of the movement of Y.

Table 3–2 contains the information on drink sales needed to compute the coefficient of determination. The expected value of Y for each set of X and Z values appears in column 6;[3] the difference between the actual and expected Y appears in column 7; and its square appears in column 8. The variance of Y around its mean appears in column 5. Based on these numbers, the coefficient of determination is

[2]For example

$$\hat{Y}_1 = 39.1953 + 9.0641 \cdot 30 + 9.6074 \cdot 12 = 426$$

$$R^2 = 1 - \frac{26^2}{12,995} = 0.948$$

Thus, the model with two independent variables explains 94.8 percent of the variance in drink sales, compared to only 74 percent for the simple regression model.

Correlation Coefficient

The multiple correlation coefficient is redundant to the coefficient of determination for multiple regression. It does not carry a plus or minus sign and is simply the square root of the coefficient of determination. It provides no new information. While some computer programs give the coefficient of determination, others give the multiple correlation coefficient.

Confidence Interval Estimation

Approximate confidence interval estimation also proceeds in a manner similar to that for simple regression. The confidence range formula is

$$\text{Confidence range} = \hat{Y} \pm t_p \text{SE} \sqrt{n/(n-k)} \qquad (3\text{-}7)$$

where n is the number of observations; k is the number of variables, including the dependent variable; and t_p is the value from the table of the t statistic (Appendix C) for $n-k$ degrees of freedom.

For the drink sales example, suppose we want a confidence range such that there is a 0.9 probability of actual sales falling within the range. Therefore, the value of $t_{0.10}$ for seven degrees of freedom is used. In Appendix C, this value is 1.895. Thus, the 0.90 confidence interval for drink sales is

$$\hat{Y} \pm 1.895 \cdot 26 \sqrt{10/(10-3)} = \hat{Y} \pm 59$$

This is a substantial improvement from the 0.90 confidence range of ± 121 for the simple regression model of drink sales.

REGRESSION WITH MORE THAN TWO INDEPENDENT VARIABLES

There is no conceptual difference between using two independent variables and using more than two; only the calculations become more complicated. The multiple regression model with numerous independent variables appears as follows:

$$Y = a + b_1 X_1 + b_2 X_2 + \ldots + b_n X_n$$

The coefficients b_1 through b_n are generally found by entering the observations for the dependent and independent variables into an appropriate computer program. Everything that has been said about goodness-of-fit measures and confidence interval estimation with two independent variables also applies for three or more independent variables.

USING MULTIPLE REGRESSION TO FORECAST

As with simple regression, a number of factors must be considered if the regression model is to provide good forecasting results. It is necessary to have historical data for dependent and independent variables, and it is necessary to have values of the independent variables to be used in the preparation of the forecast.

As with simple regression, caution is required when forecasting far into the future because past relationships may not continue to hold. Caution is also required when forecasting with independent variable values far outside the range of values observed in the past. The impacts of the independent variables may not be stable for all possible values. Table 3-1 contains no observations for point spreads greater than 22. A point spread of 50 may, for example, cause people to go home rather than to the refreshment stand.

Seasonality and nonlinearity are problems that are faced in multiple as well as simple regression. They can frequently be identified by plotting the residuals $(Y - \hat{Y})$ in the form of a graph and looking for a pattern. If there is a seasonal pattern in any data, it can be removed using methods discussed in Chapter 5, and regression can be performed on the adjusted data.

Autocorrelation is a problem with both multiple and simple regression. As with simple regression, the Durbin-Watson statistic is used as a check:

$$\text{DW} = \frac{\sum\limits_{t=2}^{n} (e_t - e_{t-1})^2}{\sum\limits_{t=1}^{n} e_t^2} \tag{3-8}$$

33

where

$$e_t = (Y_t - \hat{Y}_t)$$

For the drink sales problem, columns 8 and 9 of Table 3-2 provide the basis for the Durbin-Watson computation:

$$DW = 14,483/6,612 = 2.19$$

Using the rule of thumb suggested before, a Durbin-Watson statistic between 1.5 and 2.5 indicates no serious autocorrelation problem.

If an autocorrelation problem is found, it can frequently be eliminated by converting all numbers to amount of change:

y = change in drink sales from the previous period;

x = change in temperature from the previous period; and

z = change in point spread since the previous period (game).

The regression analysis would then be performed with these variables substituted for the original variables.

Multicollinearity is a problem that occurs with multiple regression, but not simple regression. Each of the independent variables is supposed to provide information about different factors, and is thus assumed to be unrelated to the other independent variables. Suppose, for example, that half-time point spread and game-end point spread were both used as independent variables. Each of these are measures of the closeness of the game; they would be related. This relationship would tend to distort the regression model and give misleading results. To avoid this problem, it is necessary to check for correlation between all independent variables to be included. As was discussed earlier, the correlation coefficient between any two variables, X and Z, is

$$r_{XZ} = \frac{\sigma_{XZ}}{\sigma_X \sigma_Z} \tag{3-9}$$

Using the numbers from Table 3-1, the correlation coefficient between independent variables X and Z is

$$r_{XZ} = \frac{71}{\sqrt{1,012}\sqrt{302}} = 0.13$$

Opinions differ as to what is *safe* with some people recommending as a rule of thumb that the absolute values of correlation coefficients between independent variables should be less than 0.75 and others recommending that they should be less than 0.50. The sign of the correlation coefficient is unimportant in applying one of these rules of thumb; −0.80 would be just as troublesome as a +0.80.

When a number of independent variables are being used, the normal practice is to set up the correlation coefficients in a correlation matrix (see Table 3-3). This particular table shows the desirable property of large correlation coefficients between the independent and dependent variables, but small correlation between the independent variables. When two independent variables are highly correlated with each other, it is necessary to remove one of them from the model.

If one is not sure which variables to include as independent variables, a correlation matrix may be constructed using all the variables under consideration. By examining the matrix, one can identify the factors that are highly correlated with the dependent variable—either positive or negative is good—but not highly correlated with each other. Independent variables that will cause multicollinearity problems can be eliminated or replaced. This process of examining the correlation matrix is a major aid in regression model development.

Finally, once a forecast has been prepared using regression analysis, the regression model needs to be periodically updated to be sure that the same relationships still hold.

RELATED TECHNIQUES

The two techniques closely related to multiple regression are *simple regression* and *nonlinear regression*. Each of these techniques is discussed in separate chapters. *Discriminant analysis* is closely related to regression analysis and is used when the dependent variable is stated as yes or no. Thus, it uses a model much like regression to forecast the occurrence or nonoccurrence of events. For a discussion of discriminant analysis, see

Klecka, William R. *Discriminant Analysis*, Beverly Hills: Sage Publishing Company, 1982.

Table 3-3
CORRELATION MATRIX FOR DRINK SALES

	Y	X	Z
Y	1.00	0.86	0.56
X		1.00	0.13
Z			1.00

PROBLEMS

1. Shown below are department store sales, disposable personal income, and unemployment rates for 1957 through 1981.

Year	Department Store Sales ($ billions)	Disposable Personal Income ($ billions)	Unemployment Rate
1957	12.0	308	4.3%
1958	12.6	317	6.8
1959	13.6	337	5.5
1960	13.9	349	5.6
1961	14.5	364	6.7
1962	15.8	384	5.6
1963	18.5	402	5.7
1964	20.8	438	5.2
1965	23.4	472	4.5
1966	26.1	508	3.8
1967	29.6	547	3.8
1968	33.3	590	3.6
1969	36.4	634	3.5
1970	37.3	691	4.9
1971	42.0	746	5.9
1972	46.6	803	5.6
1973	52.3	904	4.9
1974	55.9	998	5.6
1975	61.8	1,096	8.5
1976	68.2	1,194	7.7
1977	76.5	1,314	7.1
1978	84.5	1,474	6.1
1979	90.0	1,650	5.8
1980	94.7	1,824	7.1
1981	103.6	2,029	7.6

Prepare a multiple regression analysis.

2. Disposable personal income and unemployment were $2,172.5 billion and 9.7 percent respectively in 1982. Predict the 1982 department store sales and a 95 percent confidence interval.

3. A company that purchases heavy equipment finds its sales related to Gross National Product (GNP) and interest rates. Sales and GNP were

converted to 1972 dollars and then the period-to-period change was computed. Long–term U.S. Government bonds were used to represent the interest rate. The data appear below.

Year	Change in Constant Dollar Sales ($ millions)	Change in Constant Dollar GNP ($ billions)	Interest Rate
1962	3.9	43.7	3.95%
1963	2.7	32.2	4.02
1964	5.2	43.9	4.17
1965	8.5	52.9	4.23
1966	7.7	55.5	4.68
1967	−0.9	26.6	4.90
1968	3.2	46.7	5.33
1969	5.0	29.5	6.22
1970	−1.9	−2.0	6.75
1971	−0.6	36.8	5.94
1972	7.6	63.5	5.67
1973	13.8	68.4	6.12
1974	1.4	−8.0	6.59
1975	−1.1	−14.7	8.21
1976	5.0	66.6	7.87
1977	13.8	71.5	7.68
1978	13.8	68.9	8.46
1979	7.1	40.8	9.27
1980	−3.2	−5.4	11.22
1981	2.8	28.6	13.20

Prepare a multiple regression analysis.

4. The company in problem 3 had constant dollar sales of $120 million in 1981. Constant dollar GNP is expected to increase by $30 billion in 1982 and the interest rate is expected to be 12.5 percent. Prepare a sales forecast for 1982.

MULTIPLE REGRESSION PROGRAM

This program performs multiple regression analysis with one dependent variable and two independent variables. Because it is designed to use only the simplest BASIC language commands, it can be used with most personal computers. Despite its simplicity, the program

37

provides all the information needed for forecasting with two independent variables.

The program contains a set of sample data for the problem in Table 3-1. To use the program, simply replace this data with your own. The first datum must be the number of observations of the dependent variable. The first data set consists of the dependent variable observations. The second and third data sets consist of the first and second independent variables respectively. Observations must be entered in the same order in each data set so that the program will correctly match up observations.

```
10 DIM A(180)
20 READ N
30 FOR I = 1 TO N
40 READ A(I)
50 NEXT I
60 FOR I = 1 TO N
70 READ A(N+I)
80 NEXT I
90 FOR I = 1 TO N
100 READ A(2*N+I)
110 LET D = D + A(I)*A(I)
120 LET E = E + A(N+I)*A(N+I)
130 LET F = F + A(2*N+I)*A(2*N+I)
140 LET G = G + A(I)*A(N+I)
150 LET H = H + A(I)*A(2*N+I)
160 LET J = J + A(N+I)*A(2*N+I)
170 LET K = K + A(I)
180 LET L = L + A(N+I)
190 LET M = M + A(2*N+I)
200 NEXT I
210 LET P = D/N - (K/N)*(K/N)
220 LET Q = G/N - (L/N)*(K/N)
230 LET R = H/N - (M/N)*(K/N)
240 LET S = E/N - (L/N)*(L/N)
250 LET T = J/N - (L/N)*(M/N)
260 LET U = F/N - (M/N)*(M/N)
270 LET B = (R*T - Q*U)/(T*T - S*U)
280 LET C = (Q*T - R*S)/(T*T - S*U)
290 LET V = K/N - B*L/N - C*M/N
300 PRINT "                Y                    X
Z "
305 PRINT "MEAN          ";K/N,      L/N,      M/N
306 PRINT "STD. DEV."; SQR(P), SQR(S), SQR(U)
310 PRINT "CORR(Y,X) = "; Q/SQR(P*S)
320 PRINT "CORR(Y,Z) = "; R/SQR(P*U)
330 PRINT "CORR(X,Z) = ";T/SQR(S*U)
350 PRINT "REGRESSION COEFFICIENTS"
360 PRINT "A = "; V; "     B = "; B; "     C = "; C
370 FOR I = 1 TO N
380 LET A(I) = A(I) - V - B*A(N+I) - C*A(2*N+I)
```

```
390 IF I = 1 THEN 410
400 LET X = X + (A(I) - A(I-1))*(A(I) - A(I-1))
410 LET W = W + A(I)*A(I)
420 NEXT I
430 PRINT "COEF. OF DETERMINATION = "; (1-W/(N*P))
440 PRINT "STANDARD ERROR = "; SQR(W/N)
450 PRINT "DURBIN-wATSON = "; X/W
460 PRINT "DO YOU WANT TO FORECAST? (1=YES, 0=NO)"
470 INPUT X
480 IF X=0 THEN 999
490 PRINT "TO FORECAST, ENTER VALUES OF X AND Z"
500 INPUT X,Z
510 LET Y= V + B*X + C*Z
520 PRINT "THE PREDICTED VALUE OF Y IS ";Y
530 GOTO 460
800 DATA 10
810 DATA 430,335,520,490,470,210,195,270,400,480
820 DATA 30,21,35,42,37,20,8,17,35,25
830 DATA 12,10,22,6,8,2,9,8,6,17
999 END
```

Usage

You can store your observations in separate files rather than in the program itself by eliminating the DATA statements and changing the READ statements in accordance with your particular computer's file reading instructions.

You can also input the data from the keyboard during execution by removing the DATA statements and replacing statements 20 through 100 with the following:

```
20 PRINT "HOW MANY SETS OF OBSERVATIONS?"
25 INPUT N
27 PRINT "ENTER THE DEPENDENT VARIABLE,"
28 PRINT "    ONE OBSERVATION PER LINE"
30 FOR I = 1 TO N
40 INPUT A(I)
50 NEXT I
55 PRINT "ENTER THE FIRST INDEPENDENT VARIABLE,"
56 PRINT "    ONE OBSERVATION PER LINE"
60 FOR I = 1 TO N
70 INPUT A(N+I)
80 NEXT I
85 PRINT "ENTER THE SECOND INDEPENDENT VARIABLE,"
86 PRINT "    ONE OBSERVATION PER LINE"
90 FOR I = 1 TO N
100 INPUT A(2*N+I)
```

This program treats only two independent variables. Programs for handling more than two independent variables require matrix manipulation and therefore require instructions appropriate for a specific computer. The leading computer brands have available programs for handling multiple regression with more than two independent variables.

The first statement in the program—10 DIM A(180)—establishes space for the regression analysis. The number must be at least three times the number of observations. Thus, the value of 180 limits the program to 60 sets of observations. You can replace the 180 with a larger number if you have more than 60 observations or decrease the number if you need to reserve memory for some other use.

NONLINEAR REGRESSION AND TREND ANALYSIS

The focus of this chapter is on the techniques used when the item to be forecast is related to some other variable, though the relationship may not be linear. These methods are frequently used when the explanatory variable is time itself. Using the life expectancy figures for the United States (see Figure 4-1), one could attempt to forecast life expectancy by fitting a line to the data. An attempt to fit a straight line to the observations will make it clear that the relationship is not a linear one. Consequently, it is necessary to determine what type of curve best fits this data. The techniques discussed in this chapter are sometimes referred to as curve fitting.

One may try to fit a curve to a series of observations by drawing a graph (see Figure 4-1) and then fitting a curve to it by free hand drawing. This is done frequently, sometimes with considerable success.

A second approach to curve fitting is to find a mathematical formula for a curve that fits the data. When this second approach is used, the forecaster compares observations to a number of mathematical formulas that can be converted to linear form. As an example of conversion to linear form, consider a case in which Y, the item to be forecast, is related to X in the following way:

$$Y = a + b/X \qquad (4\text{-}1)$$

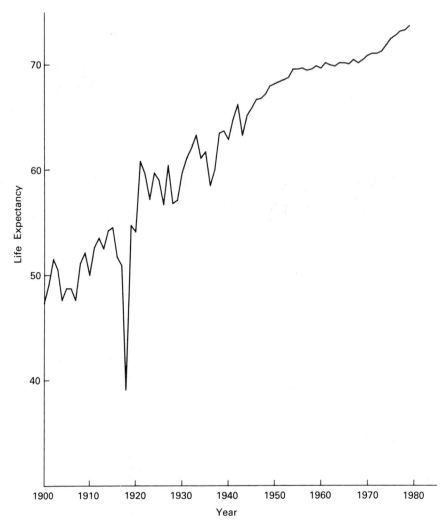

FIGURE 4–1 Life Expectancy at Birth in the United States (*SOURCE: Historical Statistics of the United States.* U.S. Department of Commerce)

If *a* and *b* are constants, both greater than zero, the graph of this relationship would appear as in Figure 4-2.

Because the relationship is not a straight line, *a* and *b* cannot be found by regression methods. Suppose, however, the values of *X* are replaced with values of $1/X$ and the equation is rewritten as

$$Y = a + b(1/X) \qquad (4\text{-}2)$$

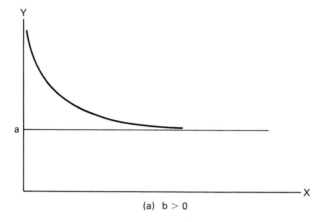

(a) b > 0

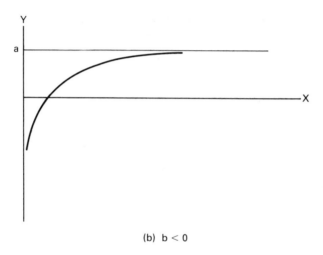

(b) b < 0

FIGURE 4-2 Inverse Linear Relationship

Using $1/X$ as the independent variable, the relationship is linear, as is shown in Figure 4-3.

Using $1/X$ as the independent variable, simple regression can be used to find the values of the coefficients a and b. In addition to the convenience of using regression to find the coefficients, conversion to linear form makes possible the use of the same goodness-of-fit tests used with simple regression analysis.

If a nonlinear relationship is suspected, the forecaster generally loads the data into a computer program such as the one at the end of

43

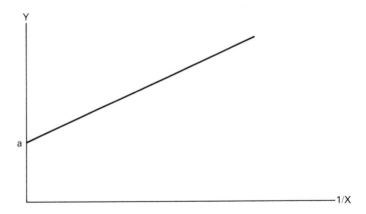

FIGURE 4-3 Inverse Linear Curve Converted to Linear Form

this chapter. That program fits each of five widely used formulas for a line to the data and checks each for goodness of fit. The program displays the goodness-of-fit measure and coefficients for each formula. The coefficients for the formula with the best fit can then be used to forecast.

TYPES OF RELATIONSHIPS

Five widely recognized types of relationships or formulas are described in this section. The situations in which the particular relationship might be observed are then identified.

Linear Pattern

The linear pattern is the simplest type to understand and use. The mathematical formula for a linear pattern is

$$Y = a + bX \qquad (4\text{-}3)$$

where

Y = the dependent variable, or the variable to be forecast;

X = the independent variable, to which Y is related;

a = the expected value of Y if X is zero; and

b = the expected change in Y for each unit change in X.

The linear relationship is, of course, the relationship used in simple regression analysis. If one were attempting to fit a straight line to the data from Figure 4-1, *b* would be the slope of the straight line drawn to fit the data, and *a* would be the expected value of *Y* when *X* is zero.

When a trend is being evaluated, *X* represents time. For example, X_1 would equal 1, X_2 would equal 2, etc.

In practical situations, few long-term trends are linear; the change per period is generally either increasing or decreasing over time. However, the linear trend approximation is frequently accurate enough for forecasts covering only a few months into the future. A linear trend estimate is also useful when the trend is overshadowed by seasonal factors. If the linear trend estimate is updated each month, errors resulting from a failure to identify the proper type of trend are likely to be small.

The Inverse Linear Pattern

The inverse linear trend follows the form

$$Y = a + b(1/X) \qquad (4\text{-}4)$$

Production cost per unit is a good example of this curve. Suppose variable cost per unit of production is *a* and total fixed costs associated with having the factory open are *b*. If *X* is the number of units produced and *Y* is unit production cost, then unit production costs will follow the inverse linear pattern of formula 4-4. The graph of this relationship would look like Figure 4-2(a).

As demonstrated on page 42, the inverse linear pattern can be readily converted to a linear pattern by simply replacing *X* with $1/X$.

Exponential (Compound Growth) Pattern

The exponential growth pattern occurs when *Y* follows a percentage growth rather than a unit growth pattern. The formula for the exponential growth pattern is

$$Y = k + a \cdot b^X \qquad (4\text{-}4a)$$

This pattern is particularly prevalent when time is the independent variable. In this case, *b* is the expected ratio of $(Y_t - k)/(Y_{t-1} - k)$. Typical shapes of the exponential growth pattern are shown in Figure 4-4.

The exponential growth pattern accurately reflects a number of real-world situations. Population and gross national product generally exhibit compound growth. Some series, such as sales of a product

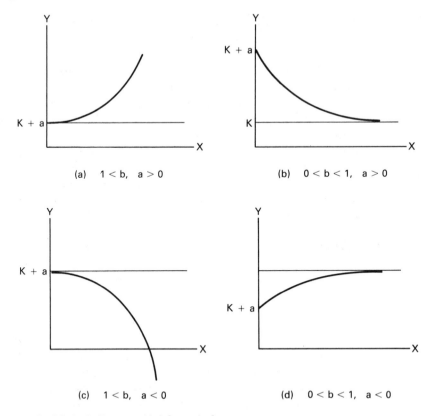

FIGURE 4-4 Exponential Growth Curves

toward the end of the product's life cycle, continue to approach zero or some other lower limit without ever reaching it [see Figure 4-4(b)]. The exponential pattern can also be used to describe growth which slows as it reaches some upper limit [see Figure 4-4(d)].

Because of its relative simplicity and its ability to accurately describe many types of patterns observed in business and economics, the exponential growth pattern is another pattern frequently assumed for short-term forecasting when seasonal and other cyclical factors are also important.

The Modified Exponential Curve

The modified exponential pattern is another exponential form, somewhat similar to the compound growth curve. Its formula is

$$Y = k + aX^b \tag{4-5}$$

Note that this pattern differs from the compound growth pattern in that X is raised to the power b rather than the other way around. The graph of the curve appears in Figure 4-5. It is similar to the exponential growth pattern, and gives the forecaster another possible curve to check for fit.

Logistic Curve

Many trends are S-shaped, starting with a low rate of growth followed by accelerating growth and then decelerating growth as the limit is approached. The logistic curve is a widely used S-shaped curve. The formula for the logistic curve is

$$Y = 1/(1/k + a \cdot b^X) \qquad (4\text{-}6)$$

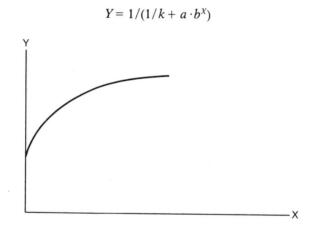

(a) $0 < a,\ 0 < b < 1$

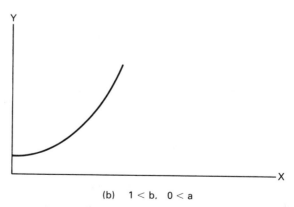

(b) $1 < b,\ 0 < a$

FIGURE 4-5 Modified Exponential Curve

where

k = the upper limit on growth;

a = a constant, normally less than 1.0; and

b = a constant, normally less than 1.0.

A sample logistic curve appears in Figure 4-6(a).

A logistic curve can be used to represent sales of a new product that exhibit slow growth during early periods followed by rapid growth and then slow growth again as saturation is reached. The k value used is normally determined from other information. To determine the percentage of families that will eventually purchase video tape equipment, one might study past sales of home entertainment products having similar characteristics. Nonlinear regression would then be used to estimate the a and b values of the logistic curve.

The logistic curve can also be used to represent a product life cycle curve. If Y represents cumulative sales of a product, the change in Y for a period represents sales during that period. Figure 4-6(a) shows cumulative sales for a product, represented as a traditional

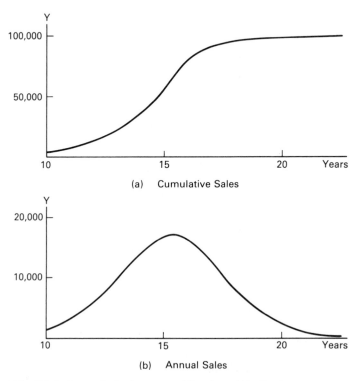

FIGURE 4-6 Logistic Curve and Product Life Cycle

S-shaped curve, and Figure 4-6(b) represents annual sales of the product following a typical product life cycle curve.

You should be cautioned against undue trust in logistic curves. While there are some natural economic and biological laws leading to the exponential growth trend, there are no laws leading to any particular S-shaped curve, although there are factors leading to S-shaped curves in general. Attempts to discover factors leading to predictable general rates of new product acceptance have not been successful. Errors are particularly likely when attempting to forecast all of the parameters of the logistic curve, including k, from observations of the early parts of the product's life cycle.

ANALYZING AND PROJECTING NONLINEAR RELATIONSHIPS

Fitting Data to Curves

Having introduced the various types of patterns, the next step is to decide which type of trend best describes the data being examined. Following this, a forecast can be prepared.

To estimate a and b through regression analysis, it is first necessary to convert the formula to its linear form. The linear form for each of the patterns is shown below:

Curve Type	Original Form	Linear Conversion
Linear	$Y = a + bX$	$Y = a + bX$
Inverse linear	$Y = a + b/X$	$Y = a + b(1/X)$
Compound growth	$Y = k + a \cdot b^X$	$\log(Y-k) = \log(a) + \log(b) \cdot X$
Modified exponential	$Y = k + a \cdot X^b$	$\log(Y-k) = \log(a) + b \cdot \log(X)$
Logistic	$Y = 1/(1/k + a \cdot b^X)$	$\log(1/Y - 1/k) = \log(a) + \log(b) \cdot X$

Generally, the computer is used to automatically compute the linear forms, find the coefficients a and b for each, and prepare goodness-of-fit measures. The calculations for fitting one curve—the exponential growth curve—are shown in Table 4-1 as an illustration of what the computer does. As pointed out earlier, the exponential growth equation is

$$Y = k + a \cdot b^X \qquad (4\text{-}7)$$

and its linear form is

$$\log(Y-k) = \log(a) + \log(b) \cdot X \qquad (4\text{-}8)$$

In the example in Table 4-1, time is the independent variable, so X simply has values of one through twelve for the twelve observations. In this example, k is set equal to zero, so $Y = Y - k$. Y must be replaced by the logarithm of Y, which appears in column 2 and is denoted Y'. Y' is used as the dependent variable and simple regression is carried out, as was done in Chapter 2.

Once the regression is completed, however, an additional adjustment is needed. The regression coefficients denoted b' and a' (see Table 4-1) are for the linear form in equation 4-8 rather than for the original form in equation 4-7. Thus, they are the logarithms of the coefficients of the original equation. The coefficients for the original equation are found by raising 2.71828 to a power equal to the coefficient of the linear form.[1]

Table 4-1
LEAST SQUARES FIT OF AN EXPONENTIAL TREND

Y	X	Y'	$(X-\overline{X})^2$	$(X-\overline{X})(Y'-\overline{Y'})$	$\hat{Y}$	$(Y-\hat{Y})^2$
7,479	1	8.91986	30.25	1.26923	7,455.38	558
8,007	2	8.98807	20.25	0.73149	7,779.24	51,874
8,135	3	9.00393	12.25	0.51343	8,117.17	318
8,077	4	8.99678	6.25	0.38462	8,469.79	154,281
8,946	5	9.09896	2.25	0.07749	8,837.71	11,722
9,364	6	9.14463	0.25	0.00300	9,221.63	20,271
9,493	7	9.15831	0.25	0.00384	9,622.22	16,697
10,057	8	9.21602	2.25	0.09810	10,040.20	282
10,434	9	9.25283	6.25	0.25550	10,476.40	1,794
10,494	10	9.25856	12.25	0.37777	10,931.40	191,319
11,610	11	9.35962	20.25	0.94049	11,406.30	41,489
12,209	12	9.40993	30.25	1.42618	11,901.80	94,371
Sum	78	109.80750	143.00	6.08114		585,426
Sum/12	6.5	9.15063	11.91667	0.50676		48,785

Standard Error $= \sqrt{48,785} = 221$

$b' = 0.50676/11.91667 = 0.042525; \quad b = 2.71828^{0.042525} = 1.04344$

$a' = 9.150629 - 0.04253 \cdot 6.5 = 8.874184; \quad a = 2.71828^{8.874184} = 7,145$

[1] The base of the system of natural logarithms is 2.71828. In other words, we are taking the antilog of a' and b'.

$$a = 2.71828^{a'} = 2.71828^{8.874184} = 7{,}145$$

$$b = 2.71828^{b'} = 2.71828^{0.042525} = 1.04344$$

Thus, the compound growth curve that fits this set of observations is

$$Y = 7{,}145 \cdot 1.04344^X$$

Using this curve, the forecast for period 13 would be

$$Y = 7{,}145 \cdot 1.04344^{13} = 12{,}419$$

The computer program computes the coefficients for each curve and then performs a goodness-of-fit test for each curve. The most widely used approach is to compute the standard error, as was done for linear regression. This is done for the compound growth curve in Table 4-1.

As shown in Table 4-1, the standard error for the exponential growth curve is 221. This standard error would be compared to the standard errors from other curves. Table 4-2 contains the computer input and output for a least squares fit of this data using all five curve types. One might continue the analysis by rerunning the tests using various values of k to see if a different k reduces the standard error.

By the standard error measure, the exponential growth curve provides the best fit. The forecast for period 13 would then be

$$7145.29 \cdot 1.04344^{13} = 12{,}419.3$$

Table 4-2
COMPUTERIZED CURVE FITTING

```
READY
>500 DATA 12,0
>510 DATA 7479,8007,8135,8077,8946,9364
>520 DATA 9493,10057,10434,10494,11610,12209
>530 DATA 1,2,3,4,5,6,7,8,9,10,11,12
>RUN

CURVE FITTING
K=0
```

CURVE	A	B	STD. ERROR
Y = A + B*X	6884.12	406.353	268.98
Y = A + B/X	10577.2	−4067.26	994.456
Y = K + A*B↑X	7145.29	1.04344	220.776
Y = K + A*X↑B	6874.75	.189129	560.949

Applications of Curve Fitting

Curve fitting is an easy-to-use forecasting method, requiring observations on only the dependent variable and on one independent variable. Its usefulness results from the fact that many relationships are nonlinear in practice. Curve fitting is particularly useful when time is the independent variable. The only data needed are observations on the independent variable. As illustrated in Figure 4-1, many growth patterns are not linear over time and can be forecast more accurately with a curve fitting method than with simple linear regression.

Frequently, data contain seasonal patterns that repeat themselves on a regular cycle. If one is attempting to fit a curve to monthly data and there is a seasonal pattern, errors are likely to result. The problem can frequently be alleviated by using methods discussed in Chapter 5 to remove the seasonal pattern.

As with other regression methods, curve fitting is based on the assumption that the pattern that existed in the past will continue in the future. The goodness-of-fit tests give only an indication of how well a particular curve fits past data. These tests leave unanswered the question of whether or not the same pattern will continue in the future. By testing a large number of curves, an accidental fit might be found for a particular time period, but examination of more time periods might reveal a completely different pattern. Companies have gone bankrupt because they studied early stages of an S-shaped curve and assumed it was a simple exponential growth curve. Intervening changes in the environment or economy such as wars, strikes, and resource shortages can cause abrupt changes in previously established patterns.

To move from a curve fitting to a forecast, the forecaster must apply all of his knowledge about the series being studied to determine the likelihood that the past pattern will continue. He must also consider the likelihood of intervening changes in the environment or economy and their influence on the series. The longer the forecast period, the more important these considerations become. While it is not uncommon to see curve fitting used to forecast trends many years into the future, the hazards in doing so are substantial.

RELATED TECHNIQUES

Multiple regression is an alternative to curve fitting, but the ability to deal with nonlinear relationships is more restricted when using multiple regression.

If curve fitting is being used to study a trend, the time series methods in Chapters 5, 6, and 7 are alternatives. If the data contains a seasonal or other cyclical pattern, it is important that one of these other methods be used prior to trend analysis, either as an alternative method or to remove the cyclical effect.

PROBLEMS

Shown below are total federal, state and local government expenditures as a percentage of Gross National Product.

FEDERAL, STATE, AND LOCAL GOVERNMENT EXPENDITURES AS A PERCENTAGE OF GROSS NATIONAL PRODUCT

Year	Percent	Year	Percent	Year	Percent	Year	Percent
1929	9.96	1950	21.31	1960	26.96	1970	31.75
1933	19.18	1951	23.99	1961	28.49	1971	32.02
1939	19.38	1952	27.04	1962	28.47	1972	31.67
1940	18.40	1953	27.75	1963	28.22	1973	30.99
1941	23.06	1954	26.48	1964	27.73	1974	32.43
1942	40.43	1955	24.54	1965	27.29	1975	34.86
1943	48.59	1956	24.84	1966	28.37	1976	33.55
1944	48.93	1957	26.04	1967	30.44	1977	32.95
1945	43.66	1958	28.43	1968	30.96	1978	31.48
1946	21.76	1959	26.93	1969	30.53	1979	31.05
1947	18.26					1980	33.09
1948	19.49					1981	33.55
1949	22.98					1982	35.47

1. Adjust or smooth the series to eliminate the impacts of major dislocations such as World War II.

2. What type of curve does this series appear to fit best?

3. Estimate the parameters of the curve used as the answer to problem 2 using the least squares method.

4. Complete a goodness-of-fit analysis.

5. Prepare a forecast for each of the five years following 1982. Identify any judgmental factors you used to supplement the statistical analysis in preparing this forecast.

6. Compare the actual figures with the forecasts for any years for which actual figures are available. (The GNP and total government expenditure figures were taken from the *Economic Report of the President.*)

Below are total population figures for the United States.

TOTAL POPULATION OF THE UNITED STATES
(IN THOUSANDS)

Year	Population	Year	Population	Year	Population
1790	3,929	1890	63,056	1971	207,100
1800	5,297	1900	76,094	1972	208,800
1810	7,224	1910	92,407	1973	210,400
1820	9,618	1920	106,461	1974	211,900
1830	12,901	1930	123,188	1975	213,600
1840	17,120	1940	132,122	1976	215,100
1850	23,261	1950	151,684	1977	216,600
1860	31,513	1960	180,671		
1870	39,905	1970	204,879		
1880	50,262				

1. What type of curve appears to fit this series best?

2. Estimate the parameters of the curve used as the answer to problem 1.

3. Complete a goodness-to-fit analysis.

4. Prepare a population forecast for the five years following 1977.

5. Compare the actual figures with the forecasts for the years for which actual data is available.

Old Reliable Life Insurance Company specializes in whole life policies, endowment policies, and other types of permanent life insurance. In a recent speech, the president of Old Reliable indicated that he felt very fortunate to be in an industry that was growing much faster than the 3 to 5 percent growth rate of the economy in general. Below are statistics on the insurance business. (All dollar figures are in billions.)

Year	Permanent Life Insurance in Force*	Total Life Insurance in Force	Consumer Price Index
1977	$895.5	$2,582.8	181.5
1976		2,343.1	170.5
1975		2,139.6	161.2
1974	697.0	1,985.1	147.7
1973		1,778.3	133.1

(*continued on next page*)

Year	Permanent Life Insurance in Force*	Total Life Insurance in Force	Consumer Price Index
1972		1,628.0	125.3
1971		1,503.3	121.3
1970	525.7	1,402.1	116.3
1969		1,284.5	109.8
1968		1,183.4	104.2
1967		1,079.8	100.0
1966	396.1	984.6	97.2
1965		900.6	94.5
1964		797.8	92.9
1963		730.6	91.7
1962	295.5	676.0	90.6
1957	211.1	458.4	84.3
1950	130.9	234.2	72.1

*Available only for selected years.

1. Is Old Reliable in a high-growth line of business?

2. Forecast total life insurance in force for the next two years.

3. Forecast permanent life insurance in force for the next two years.

4. Old Reliable has held a nearly steady 4.7 percent of the whole life market for a number of years. Forecast life insurance in force for Old Reliable for the next two years.

CURVE FITTING PROGRAM

This program fits a series of observations on dependent variable (Y) and an independent variable (X) to each of five different curves using the least squares approach of simple linear regression. The five curves are

1. $Y = a + b \cdot X$

2. $Y = a + b/X$

3. $Y = k + a \cdot b^X$

4. $Y = 1/(1/k + a \cdot b^X)$

5. $Y = k + a \cdot X^b$

The program provides a goodness-of-fit test so that you can determine which curve best fits the data. The program uses linear conversions, such as the logarithm of *Y* instead of *Y*, to determine the parameters *a* and *b*. However, the goodness-of-fit tests are based on actual and predicted values of *Y*, not on actual and predicted values of the conversion. Thus, the standard error measures can be used directly to compare the goodness of fit of the various curves.

The program includes statements using logarithms. A few very simple personal computers do not have logarithm functions and will not be able to use this program.

The program contains the data appearing in Table 4-1 and used as an example in this chapter. To use the program, simply replace these data with your own. The first data set consists of the number of sets of observations and your estimate of *k*, in that order. You may use a *k* of zero, but you must provide some value. The next data set consists of the observations on the dependent variable. The final data set consists of observations on the independent variable. The observations on the independent variable must be entered in the same order used for the dependent variable so that the computer can pair them correctly for the analysis. If time is the independent variable, the digits 1, 2, 3, etc. can be entered as the independent variable observations.

```
10 DIM D(60),I(60),A(5),B(5)
20 PRINT "CURVE FITTING"
30 READ N,K
35 PRINT "K = ";K
36 PRINT
40 FOR J=1 TO N
50 READ D(J)
60 NEXT J
70 FOR J= 1 TO N
80 READ I(J)
90 NEXT J
100 PRINT "CURVE                    A              B
STD. ERROR"
110 FOR C = 1 TO 5
120 IF K=0 AND C=4 THEN 125
123 GOTO 130
125 PRINT "CANNOT DO CURVE 4 WHEN K=0."
126 C=C+1
130 M=0
140 P=0
150 Q=0
160 R=0
170 S=0
180 FOR J = 1 TO N
190 Y = D(J)
200 X = I(J)
201 IF C=3 AND Y-K<0 THEN 485
```

```
202 IF K=0 THEN 204
203 IF C=4 AND (1/Y - 1/K)<0 THEN 485
204 IF C=5 AND Y-K<0 THEN 485
205 IF C=5 AND X<0 THEN 485
210 IF C=2 THEN X = 1/X
220 IF C=3 THEN Y = LOG(Y-K)
230 IF C=4 THEN Y = LOG(1/Y - 1/K)
240 IF C=5 THEN Y = LOG(Y-K)
250 IF C=5 THEN X = LOG(X)
260 M = M + X*Y
270 P = P+X
280 Q = Q + Y
290 R = R + X*X
300 NEXT J
310 B(C)= (N*M - P*Q)/(N*R - P*P)
320 A(C)= Q/N - B(C)*P/N
330 IF C>2 THEN A(C)= EXP(A(C))
340 IF C=3 OR C=4 THEN B(C)= EXP(B(C))
350 FOR J = 1 TO N
355 X = I(J)
360 IF C=1 THEN F = A(C)+ B(C)*X
370 IF C=2 THEN F = A(C)+ B(C)/X
380 IF C=3 THEN F = K + A(C)*B(C)[X
390 IF C=4 THEN F = 1/(1/K + A(C)*B(C)[X)
400 IF C=5 THEN F = K + A(C)*X[B(C)
410 S = S + (F-D(J))↑2
420 NEXT J
430 S = SQR(S/N)
440 IF C=1 THEN PRINT "1 Y = A + B*X",A(1),B(1),S
450 IF C=2 THEN PRINT "2 Y = A + B/X",A(2),B(2),S
460 IF C=3 THEN PRINT "3 Y = K + A*B↑X",A(3),B(3),S
470 IF C=4 THEN PRINT "4 Y = 1/(1/K + A*B↑X)"
480 IF C=4 THEN PRINT "                  ",A(4),B(4),S
483 IF C=5 THEN PRINT "5 Y = K + A*X↑B",A(5),B(5),S
484 GOTO 490
485 PRINT "CANNOT DO CURVE"; C
486 PRINT "OBSERVATION ";J;"  REQUIRES THE LOG OF A
NEGATIVE NUMBER"
490 NEXT C
500 PRINT "ENTER THE CURVE YOU WISH TO USE TO FORECAST"
510 PRINT "   (0 MEANS STOP)"
520 INPUT C
530 IF C=0 THEN 999
534 IF C=4 AND K=0 THEN 537
535 GOTO 540
537 PRINT "CANNOT DO CURVE 4 WHEN K=0"
538 GOTO 500
540 PRINT "ENTER THE VALUE OF THE INDEPENDENT VARIABLE."
550 INPUT X
560 IF C=1 THEN LET F = A(1) + B(1)*X
570 IF C=2 THEN LET F = A(2) + B(2)/X
580 IF C=3 THEN LET F = K + A(3)*B(3)↑X
590 IF C=4 THEN LET F = 1/(1/K + A(4)*B(4)↑X
593 IF C<5 THEN 610
```

```
595 IF X>=0 THEN 600
596 PRINT "CANNOT USE CURVE 5 WITH A NEGATIVE VALUE"
597 GOTO 500
600 IF C=5 THEN LET F = K + A(5)*X↑B(5)
610 PRINT "PREDICTED VALUE OF INDEPENDENT VARIABLE = ";F
620 GOTO 500
800 DATA 12,0
810 DATA 7479,8007,8135,8077,8946,9364
820 DATA 9493,10057,10434,10494,11610,12209
830 DATA 1,2,3,4,5,6,7,8,9,10,11,12
999 END
```

Application

Several of the linear conversions involve the use of logarithms. Since it is not possible to compute the logarithm of a negative number, the program checks for this difficulty. If the logarithm of a negative number would be required, a message is displayed and that particular curve type is skipped in the analysis.

You may want to store data in files other than in the program itself. This is easily accomplished by eliminating the **DATA** statements and changing the **READ** statements according to your particular computer's file reading instructions.

You can also enter the data from the keyboard during execution by replacing statements 30 through 80 with the following:

```
30 PRINT "ENTER THE NUMBER OF OBSERVATIONS"
32 INPUT N
34 PRINT "ENTER K"
35 INPUT K
38 PRINT "ENTER VALUES OF THE DEPENDENT VARIABLE,"
39 PRINT "     ONE OBSERVATION PER LINE"
40 FOR J = 1 TO N
42 INPUT D(J)
50 NEXT J
60 PRINT "ENTER THE VALUES OF THE INDEPENDENT VARIABLE,"
61 PRINT "     ONE OBSERVATION PER LINE"
70 FOR J = 1 TO N
80 INPUT I(J)
```

The first statement in the program—10 DIM D(60), I(60), A(5), B(5)—establishes space for the analysis. The values of "D(60) and I(60)" limit the program to a maximum of 60 pairs of observations. These numbers must be changed if more observations are used. Suppose, for example, sales for each of ninety-six months are being used as the independent variable. The first statement should be changed as follows:

10 DIM D(96), I(96), A(5), B(5)

5

DECOMPOSITION ANALYSIS

Like other time series techniques, decomposition methods use the history of a particular series of data to forecast future values of the series. Decomposition analysis is used primarily when the series displays some regular seasonal pattern. For example, a sporting goods retailer might use decomposition analysis to forecast monthly sales for the next year, or a manufacturer might use decomposition analysis of past sick leave experience to predict the seasonal pattern for the coming year. In addition, decomposition techniques are used to develop insights concerning a time series prior to deciding on a forecasting method.

Decomposition analysis is also used to prepare data for other types of forecasting. It is frequently necessary to remove the seasonal component from data before they can be used in analysis. Economic information, such as the unemployment rate, is frequently reported on a *deseasonalized* basis. This means that a form of decomposition has been used to identify and adjust for seasonal influences. This chapter covers the use of decomposition analysis for both deseasonalizing and forecasting.

Decomposition methods are among the easiest time series methods to understand as well as the easiest to use when a single forecast is needed. When repeated forecasts are needed, other techniques such as exponential smoothing are more economical to use.

TIME SERIES COMPONENTS

A time series can be viewed as a collection of several components. A typical time series may contain a trend component and an irregular component. In addition, it may contain seasonal or other cyclical components. The sales pattern for replacement automobile batteries, represented by the solid line, is an example of a time series with seasonal, irregular, and trend components (see Figure 5-1). Decomposition analysis involves the estimation of the various components and possibly the preparation of forecasts based on these estimates. The components are discussed in more detail in the following paragraphs.

Trend represents the long-term movements of a series. The dashed line in Figure 5-1 represents an estimate of the trend line prepared using methods discussed in this chapter. While the trend line may take on any of a number of different shapes, linear and percentage growth trends are the most widely used. A linear (straight line) trend is

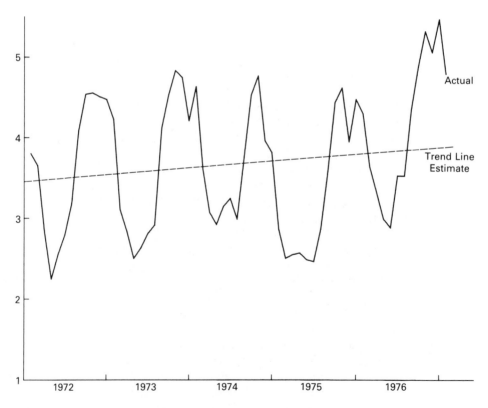

FIGURE 5-1 Replacement Auto Battery Sales (millions)

characterized by a constant unit increase or decrease each period. If battery sales were expected to increase by $12 million each year, the trend is linear. If, on the other hand, sales were expected to increase 3 percent each period, a percentage growth trend would be in evidence. A linear trend model is generally used because it is easier to apply. Due to the short-term nature of most time series forecasts, the difference in results is not usually substantial. The examples in this chapter use linear trend analysis.

Cyclical movement is typical of many time series. The most widely observed cyclical movement is seasonal, with certain patterns repeating themselves over an annual cycle. In addition to such obvious items as snow ski, lawn mower, and turkey sales, many not so obvious things move in an annual cycle: births, clothing sales, and violent crimes. In some cases, the sole objective of time series analysis may be the identification and forecasting of seasonal patterns. A company using regression to forecast annual sales may rely on decomposition analysis to estimate seasonal patterns and prepare monthly plans.

Other cyclical patterns may have lengths of more than or less than one year. New auto sales have been characterized as having a cycle of about three years in length, with one surge in sales being followed by a surge several years later as those cars are traded for new ones. In addition to the three-year cycle and seasonal pattern, auto sales follow a weekly cycle with some days of the week counting for a disproportionate share of sales.

Cyclical components may be either ratio or additive. A ratio model is one in which January sales are expected to be 20 percent above average monthly sales. An additive model is one in which January sales are expected to be $7,000 above average monthly sales. If the trend line estimate for January was $40,000, the sales forecast for January would be $40,000(1 + 0.2) = $48,000 using a ratio model, and $40,000 + $7,000 = $47,000 using an additive model. The difference between the two can be significant when the trend is large. If the trend line forecast for the following January is $70,000, the January forecast will be $70,000(1 + 0.2) = $84,000 using a ratio model, and $70,000 + $7,000 = $77,000 using an additive model. The ratio component is the more common and widely used. However, in cases where there is a negative value during some parts of the cycle, such as a profit pattern in which the company frequently experiences a loss during one part of the year, a ratio model does not behave well mathematically, and an additive model must be used.

Occasionally, a time series will contain more than one cyclical component, such as an annual cycle and a three-year cycle. The added complication is not unduly burdensome. Examples with two cyclical components are included in this chapter.

Irregular components of a time series are those occurring in a random fashion. Low auto sales for a particular September might be attributed to the unseasonably cool and rainy weather which caused many potential customers to delay their trips to the showrooms. An objective of decomposition analysis is the separation of trend and cyclical components from irregular components.

The actual value of a time series at a particular time (Y) is the product[1] of all three components:

$$Y = \text{trend line} \cdot \text{cyclical component} \cdot \text{irregular component}$$

Of course, the components are not observed separately; one sees only the values of Y. The forecaster attempts to isolate the components by first isolating the cyclical components and then estimating the trend component.

SIMPLE DECOMPOSITION

Simple decomposition is used with data having one cyclical component, such as an annual cycle. Although the method is explained using monthly data and a seasonal pattern, it can be readily applied with any cycle length. The steps involved are outlined below, and are all carried out by the computer program at the end of this chapter.

1. For each month, compute an average of the data for the twelve-month period of which that month is the center. This is called a twelve-month moving average. As an example, the twelve-month moving average on which July, 1972 is centered would include six months on either side of the middle of July—January 15, 1972 to January 15, 1973. The data in Table 5-1 are used to illustrate the computation. Since only data for complete months are given, the July, 1972 moving average uses one-half of the January, 1972 value and one-half of the January, 1973 value:

July, 1972 twelve-month centered moving average

$$\frac{1}{12}\left[\frac{3804}{2} + 3654 + 2826 + 2249 + 2558 + 2794 + 3178 + 4086 + 4538 + 4553 + 4507 + 4473 + \frac{4226}{2}\right] = 3619$$

[1]For an additive model, Y is the sum of three components:

$$Y = \text{trend line} + \text{cyclical component} + \text{irregular component}$$

Table 5-1
DECOMPOSITION ANALYSIS OF AUTO REPLACEMENT BATTERIES

1 Refer- ence	2 t	3 Raw Data	4 Centered Moving Average	5 Ratio	6 Seasonal Compo- nent	7 Desea- sonalized Sales
72-1	1	3804			1.177	3232
2	2	3654			0.894	4087
3	3	2826			0.789	3582
4	4	2249			0.723	3111
5	5	2558			0.771	3318
6	6	2794			0.814	3432
7	7	3178	3619	0.878	0.831	3824
8	8	4086	3614	1.131	1.114	3668
9	9	4538	3592	1.263	1.228	3695
10	10	4553	3603	1.264	1.265	3599
11	11	4507	3616	1.246	1.238	3641
12	12	4473	3620	1.236	1.157	3866
73-1	13	4226	3610	1.171	1.177	3590
2	14	3108	3600	0.863	0.894	3477
3	15	2837	3601	0.788	0.789	3596
4	16	2503	3612	0.693	0.723	3462
5	17	2631	3633	0.724	0.771	3412
6	18	2807	3632	0.773	0.814	3448
7	19	2915	3638	0.801	0.831	3508
8	20	4120	3675	1.121	1.114	3698
9	21	4526	3706	1.221	1.228	3686
10	22	4830	3733	1.294	1.265	3818
11	23	4741	3772	1.257	1.238	3830
12	24	4208	3811	1.104	1.157	3637
74-1	25	4629	3832	1.208	1.177	3933
2	26	3607	3820	0.944	0.894	4035
3	27	3070	3805	0.807	0.789	3891
4	28	2920	3802	0.768	0.723	4039
5	29	3143	3766	0.835	0.771	4077
6	30	3244	3717	0.873	0.814	3985
7	31	2987			0.831	3594
8	32	3754			1.114	3370
9	33	4524			1.228	3684
10	34	4760			1.265	3763
11	35	3960			1.238	3199
12	36	3811			1.157	3924

August, 1972 twelve-month centered moving average

$$\frac{1}{12}\left[\frac{3654}{2}+2826+2249+2558+2794+3178+4086+4538+4553+4507+4473+\right.$$
$$\left.4226+\frac{3108}{2}\right] = 3614$$

The centered moving averages for periods 7 and 8—July and August of 1972—appear in column 4 of Table 5-1, along with the moving averages for the remaining months. These centered moving averages are then used in the estimation of cyclical component factors.

2. *Prepare the cyclical component estimates by comparing the actual value for each month with the centered moving average for that month.* Since the centered moving average is based on twelve months and is equally weighted with data from before and after the period in question, the moving average should be free of seasonal effects and should not be affected by trend—in relation to the actual value for that month. Therefore, the difference between the actual value for a period and the twelve-month moving average for that period can be attributed to cyclical components. The ratio of actual sales for each period to the centered moving average for that period is the first cyclical component estimate (see column 5).

With three years of data, it is possible to compute two cyclical component estimates for each month; for example, the first July estimate is 0.878 and the second is 0.801.[2] The next step is to refine the cyclical component estimate by averaging the two ratios:

Month	First Ratio	Second Ratio	Average Ratio
Jan.	1.171	1.208	1.190
Feb.	0.863	0.944	0.904
Mar.	0.788	0.807	0.798
Apr.	0.693	0.768	0.731
May	0.724	0.835	0.780
Jun.	0.773	0.873	0.823
Jul.	0.878	0.801	0.840
Aug.	1.131	1.121	1.126
Sep.	1.263	1.221	1.242
Oct.	1.264	1.294	1.279
Nov.	1.246	1.257	1.252
Dec.	1.236	1.104	1.170
Total			12.135

One additional refinement is used to improve the cyclical component estimates. The cyclical component ratios should total to the number of periods per cycle (twelve in this case).[3] The actual total was 12.135. The final adjustment consists of multiplying the average ratio for each month by 12.00/12.135 so that they will sum to 12.00. For example,

$$\text{Adjusted January factor} = 1.190 \times (12.00/12.135) = 1.177;$$

$$\text{Adjusted February factor} = 0.904 \times (12.00/12.135) = 0.894; \text{etc.}$$

The adjusted seasonal factors for all months are shown in column 6 of Table 5-1.

In some cases, the purpose of the analysis is the estimation of seasonal components. A company that forecasts annual sales by some other method may need a way to break the annual sales down into monthly sales. The forecasted annual sales can be divided by twelve, and the result can be multiplied by the seasonal component for a particular month to forecast sales for that month.

3. Deseasonalize the data. Once the seasonal component has been estimated, it can be isolated from the data. This is done by dividing the actual sales for each month by the seasonal component estimate for that month.[4] The seasonal component estimates appear in column 6, and the resulting deseasonalized sales appear in column 7. These are the estimates of sales that would have occurred each month if there had been no seasonal sales pattern.

If the purpose of the decomposition was to deseasonalize the data, the job has been completed. The deseasonalized data can now be used for whatever forecasting purpose is desired. If the purpose was to forecast directly, it is necessary to estimate the trend.

4. Trend estimation. With deseasonalized sales completed, the next step is an examination for possible trends. The trend can be estimated using the program at the end of this chapter. Alternatively, a

---

[2]For an additive model, the seasonal component estimate would be the difference between the actual value and the moving average:

$$3,178 - 3,619 = -441 \text{ for July, 1972 and}$$

$$2,915 - 3,638 = -723 \text{ for July, 1973.}$$

[3]For an additive model, the seasonal components should total to zero. The actual total is divided by the number of periods per cycle, and this figure is subtracted from the cyclical component estimate for each period to complete the refinement.

[4]If an additive model is used, the seasonal component factor for each month should be subtracted from sales.

linear trend can be computed directly with this program. Regardless of the method used, the linear trend coefficients are

$$b = 4.94, \text{ and}$$

$$a = 3{,}550$$

Put in terms of Figure 5-1, a is the point where the dashed line crosses the horizontal axis—the trend line value for December, 1971—and b is the amount by which the trend line increases each month.

5. *Preparing a forecast.* The forecasting procedure can be summarized mathematically as follows:[5]

$$F_t = (a + b \cdot t)P \tag{5-1}$$

where

F_t = the forecast for period t;

a = the value of the trend line at time zero;

b = the slope of the trend line, or the expected increase per period;

t = the number of periods from period 0 to the period for which a forecast is being prepared; and

P = the seasonal component estimate for the period for which the forecast is being made.

If one wishes to forecast sales for February, 1975 (period 38), equation 5-1 yields

$$F_{38} = (3{,}550 + 4.94 \times 38)0.894 = 3{,}342$$

DECOMPOSITION WITH TWO CYCLICAL COMPONENTS

Occasionally, data will contain more than one cycle. There may be both an annual and a three-year cycle in sales of automobiles. The decomposition analysis proceeds as before, except that cyclical decomposition must be performed twice. First, the cyclical components for the shorter cycle are treated. Then, the data with the impact

[5]For an additive model, the forecasting formula is

$$F_t = (a + b \cdot t) + \text{seasonal factor}$$

of the shortest cycle removed is used to estimate the components of the longer cycle.

The treatment for two-cycle components is illustrated in Table 5-2. The series, recorded as quarterly data, has both an annual and a three-year cycle. The calculations in the first six columns of Table 5-2 are the same as those in Table 5-1. Column 6 contains the deseasonalized data.

Next, the data from column 6 are used as the raw data for a new decomposition analysis, appearing in columns 7 through 10. The data in column 10 have both cycles removed. Linear trend analysis performed on the data in column 11 yields the trend coefficients

$$b = 4.571 \text{ and}$$
$$a = 1,001$$

To carry out the analysis of two cycles with the program at the end of this chapter, it is necessary to run the program once to remove the first cycle, and then to run the program again using the decycled data as the input or raw data.

To forecast a particular quarter, it is necessary to know where that quarter lies in both the seasonal and three-year cycle. As we arbitrarily started the three-year cycle with the first quarter of 1970, the first quarter of 1980 is the fifth quarter of a twelve-quarter cycle and the first quarter of a four-quarter cycle. The trend line estimate is prepared and then is multiplied by the cyclical factors:

$$F_{41} = (1,001 + 4.571 \times 41) \times 1.235 \times 1.102 = 1,617$$

Goodness of Fit

The same goodness–of–fit test suggested in Chapters 2 through 4 can be applied with decomposition analysis. This is illustrated in Table 5-3 using the analysis in Table 5-1. The original data appears in column 2 and the estimate for that period, based on the trend line estimate and cyclical factor estimates, appear in column 3. The squared difference between estimated and actual values appears in column 4. The standard error of 243 is found by summing column 5, dividing by the number of observations, and taking the square root.

Application of Decomposition

The primary advantages of decomposition are relative simplicity and minimal start-up time. The primary disadvantage, relative to other time

Table 5-2
TWO CYCLE DECOMPOSITION ANALYSIS

1 Refer- ence	2 Raw Data	3 Centered Moving Average	4 Ratio	5 Seasonal Compo- nent	6 Deseason- alized Data	7 Centered Moving Average	8 Ratio	9 Cyclical Compo- nent	10 Decycled Data
70-1	1136			1.102	1031			1.024	1007
2	1312			1.167	1124			1.128	996
3	975	1189	0.820	0.820	1189			1.205	987
4	1190	1234	0.964	0.911	1306			1.314	994
71-1	1418	1228	1.155	1.102	1287			1.235	1042
2	1392	1164	1.196	1.167	1193			1.156	1032
3	847	1045	0.811	0.820	1033	1031	1.002	1.014	1019
4	804	913	0.881	0.911	883	1036	0.852	0.842	1049
72-1	857	831	1.031	1.102	778	1043	0.746	0.743	1047
2	897	814	1.102	1.167	769	1053	0.730	0.720	1068
3	687	860	0.799	0.820	838	1059	0.791	0.783	1070
4	826	966	0.855	0.911	907	1063	0.853	0.838	1082
73-1	1202	1074	1.119	1.102	1091	1069	1.021	1.024	1065
2	1398	1179	1.186	1.167	1198	1074	1.115	1.128	1062
3	1056	1270	0.831	0.820	1288	1076	1.197	1.205	1069
4	1297	1310	0.990	0.911	1424	1079	1.320	1.314	1084
74-1	1455	1302	1.118	1.102	1320	1080	1.222	1.235	1069
2	1469	1226	1.198	1.167	1259	1082	1.164	1.156	1089
3	915	1098	0.833	0.820	1116	1085	1.029	1.014	1101
4	830	959	0.865	0.911	911	1091	0.835	0.842	1082
75-1	897	864	1.038	1.102	814	1098	0.741	0.743	1096
2	916	839	1.092	1.167	785	1103	0.712	0.720	1090
3	707	887	0.797	0.820	862	1109	0.777	0.783	1101
4	841	1006	0.836	0.911	923	1116	0.827	0.838	1101
76-1	1269	1129	1.124	1.102	1152	1117	1.031	1.024	1124
2	1494	1244	1.201	1.167	1280	1119	1.144	1.128	1135
3	1120	1344	0.833	0.820	1366	1123	1.216	1.205	1134
4	1346	1385	0.972	0.911	1477	1127	1.311	1.314	1125
77-1	1561	1362	1.146	1.102	1417	1133	1.251	1.235	1147
2	1528	1278	1.196	1.167	1309	1137	1.151	1.156	1132
3	908	1142	0.795	0.820	1107			1.014	1092
4	880	997	0.883	0.911	966			0.842	1147
78-1	939	911	1.031	1.102	852			0.743	1147
2	990	891	1.111	1.167	848			0.720	1178
3	758			0.820	924			0.783	1180
4	877			0.911	963			0.838	1149

Table 5-3
GOODNESS-OF-FIT ANALYSIS OF AUTO REPLACEMENT
BATTERY SALES

1 t	2 Raw Data Y	3 Expected F	4 Error $\lvert Y-F \rvert$	5 $(Y-F)^2$
1	3804	4184	380	144,400
2	3654	3183	471	221,841
3	2826	2813	13	169
4	2249	2581	332	110,224
5	2558	2756	198	39,204
6	2794	2914	120	14,400
7	3178	2979	199	39,601
8	4086	3999	87	7,569
9	4538	4414	124	15,376
10	4553	4553	0	0
11	4507	4462	45	2,025
12	4473	4176	297	88,209
13	4226	4254	28	784
14	3108	3236	128	16,384
15	2837	2859	22	484
16	2503	2624	121	14,641
17	2631	2802	171	29,241
18	2807	2962	155	24,025
19	2915	3028	113	12,769
20	4120	4065	55	3,025
21	4526	4487	39	1,521
22	4830	4628	202	40,804
23	4741	4536	205	42,025
24	4208	4245	37	1,369
25	4629	4324	305	93,025
26	3607	3289	318	101,124
27	3070	2906	164	26,896
28	2920	2667	253	64,009
29	3143	2848	295	87,025
30	3244	3010	234	54,756
31	2987	3077	90	8,100
32	3754	4130	376	141,376
33	4524	4560	36	1,296
34	4760	4703	57	3,249
35	3960	4609	649	421,201
36	3811	4313	502	252,004
SUM			6821	2,124,151

Standard Error $= \sqrt{2,124,151/36} = 243$

series techniques, is the time required to update forecasts; the entire procedure must be repeated each time a new forecast is desired. Thus, if repeated forecasts are needed, one of the smoothing techniques covered in Chapters 6 and 7 is generally used.

The most significant weakness of decomposition is one shared by all time series techniques: no outside variables are considered. Shifts in patterns are recognized only after they occur, and turning points other than cyclical turns are never recognized in advance. To overcome this problem, most successful applications allow some method of including other information that may affect the forecasts. The normal approach is to give a knowledgeable person responsibility for making adjustments in the light of new information. A tire company that uses decomposition analysis to convert the annual snow tire sales forecast to a series of monthly sales forecasts does just that. Inventory analysts adjust these forecasts with regard to weather forecasts, economic conditions, and such things as a strike at a competitor's factory.

RELATED TECHNIQUES

The smoothing methods discussed in Chapters 6 and 7 can be considered alternatives to simple decomposition. They involve greater start-up effort offset by less effort for repeat forecasts, making them ideal when repeated forecasts are required. Related techniques not covered in this text are discussed at the end of Chapter 7.

PROBLEMS

1. A speculator in grain futures would be very interested in seasonal price fluctuations. In the following table, monthly average prices for #2 hard winter wheat are given. Is there a seasonal pattern in price? If so, compute the cyclical component factors for each month. Could this information be used to trade profitably in wheat futures?

PRICES OF #2 HARD WINTER WHEAT

	1971	1972	1973	1974	1975
January	1.65	1.62	2.67	5.70	4.42
February	1.65	1.61	2.48	5.78	4.02
March	1.62	1.61	2.50	5.25	3.78
April	1.62	1.63	2.55	4.19	3.76
May	1.62	1.64	2.64	3.67	3.45

PRICES OF #2 HARD WINTER WHEAT (Continued)

	1971	1972	1973	1974	1975
June	1.64	1.53	2.79	4.30	3.40
July	1.56	1.61	2.84	4.46	4.01
August	1.56	1.86	4.71	4.36	4.31
September	1.55	2.10	5.09	4.47	4.36
October	1.58	2.18	4.72	4.92	4.29
November	1.60	2.29	4.78	4.99	3.92
December	1.60	2.60	5.23	4.84	3.79

2. Cattle producers frequently refer to the ten-year cattle cycle wherein overproduction results in low prices and decreased herd size until prices rise and producers start again to rebuild their herds, thus starting another round in the cycle. Following are cattle slaughter statistics since 1913. Can you identify a cattle cycle? As a cattle producer, how could you use this information?

INSPECTED SLAUGHTER OF BEEF
(NUMBER OF ANIMALS)

Year	Slaughter	Year	Slaughter	Year	Slaughter	Year	Slaughter
		1921	7,768	1931	8,286	1941	11,141
		1922	8,667	1932	7,663	1942	12,232
1913	6,903	1923	8,938	1933	8,800	1943	11,453
1914	6,587	1924	9,292	1934	9,770	1944	13,221
1915	6,948	1925	9,557	1935	9,011	1945	14,060
1916	8,021	1926	10,040	1936	10,412	1946	11,003
1917	9,583	1927	9,203	1937	9,372	1947	15,524
1918	10,931	1928	8,244	1938	9,381	1948	12,994
1919	9,377	1929	8,246	1939	9,353	1949	13,222
1920	8,268	1930	8,204	1940	9,660	1950	13,103
1951	11,879	1961	19,968	1971	31,419		
1952	13,165	1962	20,339	1972	32,267		
1953	17,629	1963	21,662	1973	30,521		
1954	18,476	1964	25,133	1974	33,319		
1955	19,056	1965	26,614	1975	36,904		
1956	20,186	1966	27,319	1976	38,992		
1957	19,454	1967	27,280				
1958	17,642	1968	29,592				
1959	17,458	1969	30,536				
1960	19,394	1970	30,793				

3. Allied Products uses a combination of an econometric model and executive judgment to forecast the annual sales level. The forecasts for 1981 are:

Optimistic: 15 percent growth over 1980
Most likely: 5 percent   "   "   "
Pessimistic: 5 percent decline from 1980

To complete the operating plan, these estimates must be broken down to monthly sales forecasts. Below are monthly sales data for the past four years. Based on these figures, prepare monthly sales forecasts for each of the three growth rates.

	1977	1978	1979	1980
January	27,936	32,689	29,483	30,366
February	47,430	51,939	51,134	48,906
March	71,047	70,299	76,690	76,669
April	103,716	101,510	106,155	102,202
May	148,013	147,981	140,190	143,713
June	152,576	177,495	168,105	168,988
July	181,320	196,206	178,617	194,676
August	149,269	149,229	166,452	171,029
September	114,275	125,164	132,131	128,161
October	99,785	95,030	100,546	105,396
November	84,166	80,116	79,950	86,022
December	20,646	19,334	20,201	22,478

DECOMPOSITION ANALYSIS PROGRAM

This program measures seasonal or other cyclical components in a time series and then removes the effects of cyclical variations from the data. The program is used when the seasonal factors are needed or when deseasonalized data is needed for some other forecasting method such as regression or trend analysis. One might use the deseasonalized data that is the output of this program as the input for the trend analysis program in Chapter 4.

The program contains as data the time series analyzed in Table 5-1. To use the program, you only need to replace this data with your own. The first set of data for this program consists of the number of observations, the number of periods per cycle, and a 0 or 1, depending on whether the cyclical factor is to be treated as ratio (0) or additive (1).

The second data set consists of the series of observations, entered in order from earliest to most recent. The number of observations must be at least twice the number of periods per cycle and must be a multiple of the number of periods per cycle. For example, the number of observations required for monthly data with a seasonal pattern would be 24, 36, 48, or some greater multiple of 12.

```
10 DIM A(132)
20 READ N, C, G
30 FOR I = 1 TO N
40 READ A(I)
50 NEXT I
60 LET K = C/2
70 FOR I = 2 TO C
80 LET A(N+K+1) = A(N+K+1) + A(I)/C
90 NEXT I
100 LET A(N+K+1) = A(N+K+1) + (A(1)/2 + A(C+1)/2)/C
110 FOR I = K+2 TO N-K
120 LET A(N+I) = A(N+I-1) - .5*(A(I-K) + A(I-K-1) - A(I+K)
- A(I+K-1))/C
130 NEXT I
140 FOR I = K+1 TO N-K
150 IF G=0 THEN LET A(N+I) = A(I)/A(N+I)
160 IF G<>0 THEN LET A(N+I) = A(I) - A(N+I)
170 NEXT I
180 LET M = N/C - 1
190 FOR J = 1 TO N STEP C
200 FOR I = 0 TO C-1
210 LET K = J + I
220 LET A(2*N+I+1) = A(2*N+I+1) + A(N+K)/M
230 NEXT I
240 NEXT J
250 FOR I = 1 TO C
260 T = T + A(2*N+I)
270 NEXT I
280 IF G=0 THEN LET T = T/C
290 FOR I = 1 TO C
300 IF G = 0 THEN LET A(2*N+I) = A(2*N+I)/T
310 IF G<>0 THEN LET A(2*N+I) = A(2*N+I)-T/C
320 NEXT I
330 FOR J = 1 TO N STEP C
340 FOR I = 0 TO C-1
350 LET K = J + I
360 IF G = 0 THEN LET A(N+K) = A(K)/A(2*N+I+1)
370 IF G <> 0 THEN LET A(N+K) = A(K) - A(2*N+I+1)
380 NEXT I
390 NEXT J
400 PRINT " CYCLICAL FACTORS"
410 FOR I = 1 TO C
420 PRINT I, A(2*N+I)
430 NEXT I
435 PRINT "HOW MANY LINES OF DECYCLED DATA DO YOU WANT"
```

```
436 PRINT "TO SEE AT A TIME? (0=STOP)"
437 INPUT Q
438 IF Q=0 THEN 999
440 PRINT "PERIOD        RAW DATA        DECYCLED
450 FOR I = 1 TO N
460 LET Z=Z+1
470 PRINT I, A(I), A(N+I)
480 IF I=N THEN 540
490 IF Z<Q THEN 540
510 PRINT "PRESS ENTER TO CONTINUE"
520 INPUT D
530 PRINT "PERIOD        RAW DATA        DECYCLED"
540 NEXT I
800 DATA 36, 12, 0
810 DATA 3804,3654,2826,2249,2558,2794,3178,4086,4538
820 DATA 4553,4507,4473,4226,3108,2837,2503,2631,2807
830 DATA 2915,4120,4526,4830,4741,4208,4629,3607,3070
840 DATA 2920,3143,3244,2987,3754,4524,4760,3960,3811
999 END
```

Application

Most cycles contain an even number of periods—twelve months, four quarters, etc. However, there are times when an uneven number of periods would be used: daily data with a weekly pattern would apply to restaurant sales, for example. If the number of periods per cycle is uneven, statements 60 through 140 must be replaced with the following statements.

```
60 LET K = (C+1)/2
70 FOR I = 2 TO C+1
80 LET A(N+K+1) = A(N+K+1) + A(I)/C
90 NEXT I
110 FOR I = K+2 TO N-K+1
120 LET A(N+I) + A(N+I) - A(I-K)/C + A(I+K-1)/C
130 NEXT I
140 FOR I = K+1 TO N-K+1
```

Like the other programs in this book, data can be read from a file rather than stored in the program. It is only necessary to change the READ statements according to your particular computer's file reading instructions.

Data can also be entered from the keyboard during execution. Simply remove the DATA statements and replace statements 20 through 110 with the following.

```
14 PRINT "HOW MANY OBSERVATIONS?"
16 INPUT N
18 PRINT "HOW MANY PERIODS PER CYCLE?"
20 INPUT C
22 PRINT "ARE CYCLICAL COMPONENTS RATIO OR ADDITIVE?"
23 PRINT "  (RATIO = 0, ADDITIVE = 1)"
24 INPUT G
26 PRINT "ENTER THE OBSERVATIONS, ONE LINE PER"
27 PRINT "OBSERVATION, IN ORDER FROM OLDEST TO MOST RECENT"
30 FOR I = 1 TO N
40 INPUT A(I)
```

To have the program compute the linear trend coefficients, change line 438 to

```
438 IF Q=0 THEN 550
```

and insert the following lines

```
550 FOR I = 1 TO N
560 LET R = R + I*I
570 LET S = S + A(N+I)
580 LET U = U + A(N+I)*A(N+I)
590 LET V = V + A(N+I)
600 LET B = (V/N-S*(N+1)/(2*N))/(R/N-((N+1)/2)*((N+1)/2))
610 LET F = S/N - B*(N+1)/2
620 PRINT "TREND LINE"
630 PRINT "A = ";F
640 PRINT "B = ";B
650 FOR I = 1 TO C
660 LET H = H+1
670 LET W = W+((F+H*B)A(2*N+C)-A(N+H)↑2
680 NEXT I
690 IF H<N THEN 660
700 PRINT "STANDARD ERROR = ";SQR(W/N)
```

The standard error computed here is not the same one computed in Table 5-3; it is the fit of the model to the original data, not the fit of the linear regression line to the deseasonalized data.

You may also need to change the number in parentheses in the DIM statement, which is the first statement in the program. That number must be at least twice the number of periods of data being used, plus the number of periods per cycle.

6

MOVING AVERAGE METHODS

The time series methods discussed in the previous two chapters depended on some trend line such as the linear trend:

$$Y = a + bX$$

While trend lines are useful, they have two limitations. First, they are difficult to update; it is necessary to complete the entire trend line estimate each time the forecast is to be updated. Second, because trend line estimating methods attach the same significance to all past observations, they do not respond quickly to changes in the pattern and may result in large errors when such changes occur.

The moving average methods discussed in this chapter overcome both of these problems. An example of a simple moving average forecasting method is

$$\begin{aligned} \text{Nov. sales} \atop \text{forecast} &= \frac{1}{2}\,\text{Oct. sales} + \frac{1}{4}\,\text{Sept. sales} + \frac{1}{4}\,\text{Aug. sales} \end{aligned}$$

$$\begin{aligned} \text{Dec. sales} \atop \text{forecast} &= \frac{1}{2}\,\text{Nov. sales} + \frac{1}{4}\,\text{Oct. sales} + \frac{1}{4}\,\text{Sept. sales, etc.} \end{aligned}$$

Moving average methods make possible response to changes in seasonal or growth patterns: Weights can be chosen according to the desired emphasis on more recent observations. Moreover, the moving average models can be updated much more easily than trend line estimates.

Moving average methods are commonly used when repeated forecasts are desired and are particularly useful when the pattern in the data might change over time. These are conditions frequently encountered in practical forecasting.

In this chapter, simple moving averages and some weighted moving average methods, including adaptive filtering, are covered. Chapter 7 covers exponential smoothing methods—a group of economical, widely used, weighted moving average techniques.

SIMPLE MOVING AVERAGES

A simple moving average is used when there is neither a trend nor a cyclical pattern. Thus, the forecast is an average of the last n observations:

$$F_t = \frac{1}{n} \sum_{i=1}^{n} Y_{t-i} \qquad (6\text{-}1)$$

With this form of moving average, each of the last n values is given equal weight in preparing a forecast. The only decision faced is the choice of n. If an n of 1 is used, the forecast simply equals the actual value for the previous period. If n equals 2, the forecast is the average of the values for the last two periods, etc. The greater the value of n, the less the forecast will be affected by random fluctuations. On the other hand, a high value of n causes the forecasting model to react slowly to changes in the series.

A simple moving average could be used for a series that has neither trend nor cyclical patterns. If trend or cyclical factors are present, weighted averages must be used. Because weighted moving average methods give the forecaster more flexibility in designing a forecasting model, they are frequently used, even when there is neither a trend nor cyclical pattern.

WEIGHTED MOVING AVERAGES

The group of weighted moving average techniques include some powerful and economical forecasting methods. These methods have been widely used in practice, particularly where repeated forecasts are needed. The remainder of this chapter as well as the next chapter are devoted to weighted moving average techniques.

The sum of the digits method is an easy weighted average method to use. Like the simple moving average, it is used when there is neither a trend nor a cyclical pattern. The sum of the digits method places relatively greater weight on more recent observations, allowing the model to respond quickly to any shifts in the series being studied. The sum of the digits method weights each of the last *n* observations with a value from 1 to *n*, with *n* being assigned to the most recent observation and 1 being assigned to the oldest observation:

$$F_t = \frac{nY_{t-1} + (n-1)Y_{t-2} + \ldots + 1Y_{t-n}}{1 + 2 + 3 + \ldots + n} \qquad (6\text{-}2)$$

In Table 6-1, forecasts are shown for both five-period simple moving averages and five-period sum of the digits moving averages. For example, the period 12 forecast using the sum of the digits method is computed as follows:

$$F_{12} = \frac{5(120) + 4(125) + 3(115) + 2(120) + 1(105)}{1 + 2 + 3 + 4 + 5} = 119.33$$

Table 6-1
FIVE-PERIOD SIMPLE AND WEIGHTED AVERAGE FORECASTS

t	Y_t	Simple Moving Average		Sum of the Digits Weighted Average	
		F_t	Error	F_t	Error
1	105				
2	100				
3	105				
4	95				
5	100				
6	95	101	− 6	100	− 5
7	105	99	+ 6	98	+ 7
8	120	100	+20	100	+20
9	115	103	+12	107	+ 8
10	125	107	+18	111	+14
11	120	112	+ 8	117	+ 3
12	120	117	+ 3	119	+ 1

The series in Table 6-1 illustrates the trade-off faced in all moving average techniques. While there is no general trend in this particular series, shifts may occur. Suppose a company sells to a few large customers, and there is no trend in demand. The gain or loss of one customer would cause a shift in the series. This appears to have occurred at period 8 in Table 6-1. However, this shift is obvious only in retrospect. At period 8, the higher figure could be either a shift in the series or a single unusual event, such as a one-time special sale. The method that placed more weight on recent observations adjusted to the shift more quickly. Unfortunately, it would also have resulted in a larger error if the high level in period 8 had been a one-time phenomenon. Thus, the choice of a weighting system involves a trade-off between quick response to shifts and the risk of being misled by a random fluctuation. The weighting system chosen will have a substantial impact on forecasting errors. Methods of selecting proper weights are a major part of the moving average forecasting problem. Later in this chapter, some methods of systematically arriving at optimal weights are suggested.

Trend adjustment methods can be used if a trend in the series under study is expected. The simplest such method is for the case of a linear trend:

$$F_t = Y_{t-1} + (Y_{t-1} - Y_{t-2}) \qquad (6\text{-}3)$$

For computational convenience, equation 6-3 is normally restated as

$$F_t = 2Y_{t-1} - Y_{t-2} \qquad (6\text{-}3')$$

In effect, this simple method assumes that all change is a result of trend. If there are significant random movements, large errors will result. Sensitivity to random movements can be reduced by expanding the model to include any even number of periods. If four periods are used, the forecasting equation becomes:

$$F_t = \frac{7Y_{t-1} + 7Y_{t-2} - 3Y_{t-3} - 3Y_{t-4}}{8} \qquad (6\text{-}4)$$

If six periods are used, the forecasting formula is

$$F_t = \frac{10Y_{t-1} + 10Y_{t-2} + 10Y_{t-3} - 4Y_{t-4} - 4Y_{t-5} - 4Y_{t-6}}{18} \qquad (6\text{-}5)$$

This same trend model can be expanded to include more periods of history, if desired.[1]

Example—The series in Table 6-2 obviously follows a trend of some type; the values increase fairly steadily from period to period. Forecasts were prepared using two-period, four-period, and six-period sums of the digits weighted moving averages. In this case, the two-period model is overly sensitive to random movements while the six-period model is too slow in responding to changes. The four-period moving average produces the smallest standard error.

ADAPTIVE FILTERING

The moving average techniques presented thus far have several characteristics which leave opportunities for improvement. First, they provide no method for dealing with cyclical patterns. Second, the calculations required to update the forecast each period, while not extremely time consuming, do require operations on n periods of historical data for each updating. Third, the models do not learn from past errors. That is, there is no mechanism for automatically modifying the model in response to changes in the relative importance of random movements and pattern shifts.

In the balance of this chapter and in the next, techniques that can respond to changes in the relative importance of trend, seasonal, and random factors are introduced. Adaptive filtering is one of these techniques. The method was apparently first suggested by Widrow,[2] although it owes much of its current popularity to development work by Wheelwright and Makridakis.[3]

As with all weighting methods, adaptive filtering is based on the general weighting equation:

$$F_t = w_1 Y_{t-1} + w_2 Y_{t-2} + \ldots + w_n Y_{t-n} \tag{6-6}$$

[1]The general formula for an n period model is

$$F_t = \frac{1}{k} \sum_{i=1}^{k} Y_{t-i} + \frac{k+1}{n^2} \sum_{i=1}^{n/2} Y_{t-i} - \sum_{i=n/2+1}^{n} Y_{t-i}$$

k determines the rate at which the model adjusts to shifts in the series and n determines the rate at which it adjusts to changes in trend.

[2]Widrow, Bernard. "Adaptive Filters I: Fundamentals." Stanford University Technical Report No. 67, 64–6. Systems Theory Laboratory.

[3]Wheelwright, Steven C. and Spyros Makridakis. *Forecasting Methods for Management.* New York: John Wiley, 1977.

Table 6-2
LINEAR WEIGHTED MOVING AVERAGE ANALYSIS WITH TREND PRESENT NITROGEN GAS PRODUCTION

Period	Y_t	2-Pd. Moving Ave.		4-Pd. Moving Ave.		6-Pd. Moving Ave.	
		F_t^*	Error Squared	F_t^{**}	Error Squared	F_t^{***}	Error Squared
1	15,118						
2	14,804						
3	15,899						
4	14,946						
5	15,936						
6	15,994						
7	16,411	16,052	128,881	16,372	1,521	15,860	303,601
8	16,697	16,828	17,161	16,774	5,929	16,712	225
9	16,302	16,983	463,761	16,996	481,636	16,883	337,561
10	17,260	15,907	1,830,609	16,722	289,444	17,033	51,529
11	16,827	18,218	1,934,881	16,951	15,376	17,179	123,904
12	17,316	16,394	850,084	17,452	18,496	17,082	54,756
13	17,982	17,805	31,329	17,289	480,249	17,577	164,025
14	17,307	18,648	1,798,281	18,103	633,616	17,790	233,289
15	19,205	16,632	6,620,329	18,074	1,279,161	18,027	1,387,684
16	18,404	21,103	7,284,601	18,711	94,249	18,852	200,704
17	19,512	17,603	3,644,281	19,675	26,569	18,926	343,396
18	18,691	20,620	3,721,041	19,485	630,436	20,044	1,830,609
19	19,354	17,870	2,202,256	19,324	900	19,339	225
20	19,344	20,017	452,929	19,071	74,529	19,773	184,041
21	19,425	19,334	8,281	19,534	12,100	19,189	55,696
22	19,950	19,506	197,136	19,656	86,436	19,711	57,121
23	19,243	20,475	1,517,824	19,941	487,204	19,831	345,744
24	19,862	18,536	1,758,276	19,756	11,236	19,812	2,500
Sum			34,461,941		4,629,087		5,676,610
Standard Error ($\sqrt{\text{Sum}/18}$)			1,384		507		561

*For example, $F_7 = 2(15,994) - 15,936 = 16,052$

**For example, $F_7 = [7(15,994) + 7(15,936) - 3(14,946) - 3(15,899)]/8 = 16,372$

***For example, $F_7 = [10(15,994) + 10(15,936) + 10(14,946) - 4(15,899) - 4(14,804) - 4(15,118)]/18 = 15,860$

However, adaptive filtering provides a systematic way of adjusting the weights for new information.

The technique is illustrated with quarterly automobile battery sales. Since a seasonal pattern is anticipated, it would be logical to use four or eight periods for the moving average. Four periods are used for this illustration. To recognize the seasonal factor, it would also make sense to place the most weight on the quarter four quarters prior to the quarter for which the forecast is being made.

SALES FOR 1980

Quarter	IV	III	II	I
Sales	13,533	11,802	7,601	10,284

Weights of 0.2, 0.2, 0.2, and 0.4 are arbitrarily chosen to begin with. The forecast for the first quarter of 1981 is thus:

$$0.2(13,533) + 0.2(11,802) + 0.2(7,601) + 0.4(10,284) = 10,701$$

After the first quarter of 1981, the forecast is compared to actual sales, and the weights are adjusted with the objective of improving accuracy. The formula used in adjusting the weights is:

$$w_i' = w_i + 2k[(Y_t - F_t)/y^2]Y_{t-i} \qquad (6\text{-}7)$$

where

w_i' = the updated value of weight i;

w_i = the prior value of weight i;

k = a constant that determines the rate of adjustment in values of w_i; and

y = the largest of the most recent n values of Y.

The selection of a proper value of k will be taken up shortly. For the moment, a frequently applied rule of thumb is used, setting k equal to $1/n$.

Actual sales for the first quarter of 1981 were 10,171. The updated weights are therefore:

$$w_1' = 0.2 + 2(0.25)[(10,171-10,701)/13,533^2]13,533 = 0.1804$$
$$w_2' = 0.2 + 2(0.25)[(10,171-10,701)/13,533^2]11,802 = 0.1829$$

$$w_3' = 0.2 + 2(0.25)[(10,171-10,701)/13,533^2]7,601 = 0.1890$$

$$w_4' = 0.4 + 2(0.25)[(10,171-10,701)/13,533^2]10,284 = 0.3851$$

The forecast for period six—the second quarter of 1981—is based on these new weights and the actual sales for periods 2 through 5:

$$F_6 = 0.1804(10,171) + 0.1829(13,533) + 0.1890(11,802) + 0.3851(7,601) = 9,468$$

When the actual value for period 6 becomes known, the w_i values will be updated again and a forecast for period 7 will be prepared. Table 6-3 is an extension of this process, showing the continued operation of the adaptive filtering method over twelve quarters.

Because the initial weight selection is arbitrary, a common practice is to run in the model on some historical data to adjust the weights before the first actual forecast is made. For instance, the first actual forecast might be for the first quarter of 1983, with the so-called forecasts for 1981 and 1982 being used simply to refine the weights.

Frequently, the weights are further refined by substituting the weights developed at the end of the training period—0.1681, 0.1715, 0.2543, and 0.4605 in this case—for the weights arbitrarily chosen at the beginning of the training period and repeating the training process. Frequently, this substitution and retraining process is repeated many times. Table 6-4 shows the results of repeating this analysis one

Table 6-3
ADAPTIVE FILTERING: QUARTERLY SALES OF REPLACEMENT AUTO BATTERIES

Period t	Sales Y_t	Forecast F_t	w_1	w_2	w_3	w_4
1	10,284					
2	7,601					
3	11,802					
4	13,533		0.2	0.2	0.2	0.4
5	10,171	10,701	0.1804	0.1829	0.1890	0.3851
6	7,941	9,468	0.1380	0.1265	0.1398	0.3534
7	11,561	8,445	0.2056	0.2130	0.2549	0.4538
8	13,779	12,802	0.2364	0.2342	0.2820	0.4899
9	11,306	13,187	0.1681	0.1769	0.2427	0.4395
10	9,307	10,635	0.1286	0.1287	0.2023	0.4118
11	11,265	10,200	0.1547	0.1605	0.2409	0.4442
12	12,531	12,080	0.1681	0.1715	0.2543	0.4605

Table 6-4
**TRAINING ITERATIONS FOR ADAPTIVE FILTERING ANALYSIS
OF AUTOMOBILE REPLACEMENT BATTERY SALES**

Iteration Number	Standard Error	w_1	w_2	w_3	w_4
1	1,578	0.1681	0.1715	0.2543	0.4605
2	1,441	0.1270	0.1226	0.2836	0.5067
3	1,316	0.0979	0.0728	0.2989	0.5530
4	1,208	0.0800	0.0245	0.3021	0.5975
5	1,113	0.0719	−0.0201	0.2952	0.6384
10	756	0.1264	−0.1555	0.1827	0.7605
20	431	0.2471	−0.1022	0.0531	0.7154
30	393	0.2142	−0.0643	0.0929	0.6906
40	386	0.2029	−0.0772	0.0914	0.7098
50	386	0.2049	−0.0718	0.0813	0.7120
100	383	0.1847	−0.0511	0.0660	0.7275

hundred times. Table 6-4 contains standard errors and weight values after various numbers of iterations.

As can be seen from Table 6-4, additional training iterations reduce the average forecasting error. The table also illustrates the relatively large number of iterations required before the errors approach their lowest possible level. Although the required number of iterations can be reduced through more accurate beginning estimates of the *w* values, such estimation procedures are themselves time consuming. While preparing new forecasts and updating the *w* values can be done quickly, the beginning training iterations require a large number of computations. Fortunately, these calculations can be carried out quickly using the computer program at the end of this chapter.

Initial Values of Weights

The beginning values of the weights were given in this particular problem. In practice, there are two ways to assign them. One is to assign equal value to each weight. Since four periods were being used, each weight could have been set equal to 0.25 to begin with. However, it is frequently possible to reduce the number of training iterations and improve the final accuracy of the model by giving a bit more attention to the beginning weight estimates.

Examination of the data frequently makes it possible to develop relatively good beginning weight estimates. The data in Table 6-3 represent quarterly sales. The values for the second quarter of each year were low while the fourth-quarter values were always high. Thus, it appears that there is some sort of annual cycle. With an annual cycle, one would expect the value four periods ago to be particularly important in forecasting the value for this period. Thus the initial weight for w_4 was set at twice the values of the other weights (see Table 6-3). Since no trend was immediately obvious, the total of the four weights was set equal to 1.0.

When the most important pattern appears to be a trend rather than a cyclical pattern, equations 6-3, 6-4, or 6-5 could be used to set the starting values of the weights. Using equation 6-4, the starting values would be

$$w_1 = 7/8$$
$$w_2 = 7/8$$
$$w_3 = -3/8$$
$$w_4 = -3/8$$

Number of Weights: *n*

For cyclical data, one cycle is generally used in preparing a new forecast. The data examined in Table 6-3 exhibit an annual cycle and are reported on a quarterly basis. Therefore, the forecast for each period is based on the four immediately preceding periods. For monthly data with an annual cycle, twelve periods would be used.

When no cycle is present, two to six periods are generally used. Higher values of n reduce the impact of random fluctuations, with the trade-off being that a higher n results in a slower adjustment to changes in pattern. Frequently, several values of n are tested to see which one produces the lowest average error.

Selecting the Training Constant: *k*

Like the selection of n, the selection of the training constant involves a trade-off. Higher values of k lead to rapid adjustment to changes in patterns, but also make the model more sensitive to random fluctuations. As an upper limit, k should not be set at a value higher than $1/n$, where n is the number of weights being used. With a higher k, the model may not converge on stable values for the weights. As a rule of thumb, it is common practice to simply set k equal to $1/n$. For a further refinement, alternative values of k can be tested, and the one that results in the smallest standard error can be used.

Applications of Moving Averages

As a group, the moving average methods are better than trend analysis or decomposition in adjusting to shifts in patterns. Furthermore, they are more economical to update and require less data storage. Because these advantages are somewhat offset by higher start-up costs, the moving average methods are most frequently used when repeated forecasts are needed.

The methods discussed in this chapter, with the exception of adaptive filtering, include no method for adjusting the weights in response to changing patterns. Thus, they require constant monitoring if they are to be used. The adaptive filtering method overcomes this problem by including a method for adjusting the weights each period.

The greatest potential problem with adaptive filtering arises from its method of updating weights. The approach is called the method of steepest descent; the method attempts to reduce the forecasting error on each readjustment of the weights. In certain cases, as illustrated below, the method fails to find the optimal weights.

Two simple time series illustrate the problems involved in finding optimal weights. Suppose adaptive filtering is used to analyze the following set of values: 1, 2, 3, 4, 5, 6, 7, 8, 9, 10. The optimal weights are $w_1 = 2$ and $w_2 = -1$. If we start with $n = 2$ and both weights set at 0.5, the solution will be found after a sufficient number of iterations, and the average error will decline to zero.

Suppose, instead, one were to analyze the series 101, 102, 103, 104, 105, 106, 107, 108, 109, 110. Again, the optimal weights are $w_1 = 2$ and $w_2 = -1$. Starting with $n = 2$ and both weights set at 0.5, the optimal set of weights will not be found. After fifty iterations, the model will settle in on the weights $w_1 = 0.5070$ and $w_2 = 0.5069$. This is the best set of weights that can be reached using the adaptive filtering method, and it does not result in zero error.

Because of this limitation of adaptive filtering, it is necessary to take precautions against the selection of a suboptimal model. Problems of this type can frequently be overcome by a little extra effort in selecting the beginning weights. As an extra check, it is worthwhile to compare the accuracy of the adaptive filtering model to a naive method such as a simple moving average model or a moving average model with trend assumed. Another approach is to compare results of the adaptive filtering model with the exponential smoothing model discussed in Chapter 7. This effort is frequently justifiable since moving average models are generally used when repeated forecasts are needed, and gains in accuracy will be recognized many times over. Adaptive filtering is a powerful and useful forecasting tool if this limitation is kept in mind.

RELATED TECHNIQUES

Exponential smoothing, discussed in Chapter 7, is the most closely related technique covered in this text. Exponential smoothing is a type of moving average method; it differs in the way in which weights are assigned and past data is used. Exponential smoothing is frequently less expensive to use and will give better results in some cases. It is particularly powerful when cyclical patterns are involved. One may want to try both types of models on a particular set of data to determine which gives the most accurate forecast.

=== PROBLEMS ===

1. Allied Hardware, lacking sophisticated computational equipment or trained personnel, wishes to use a weighted average method to forecast monthly sales of individual items. The store is experiencing modest sales growth and wants to use a trend adjustment weighting method. Test the two-period, four-period, and six-period formulas (equations 6-3', 6-4, and 6-5) on tool sales to determine which would have given the best forecasts in the past. Is it reasonable to assume that the method that provides the best forecasts for tools will also provide the best forecasts for garden supplies? Are there any other forecasting methods you would recommend to Allied?

TOOL SALES AT ALLIED HARDWARE

	1981	1982	1983
January	1,727	1,916	1,841
February	1,825	1,735	1,872
March	1,684	1,766	1,862
April	1,772	1,784	2,018
May	1,766	1,814	2,020
June	1,838	1,824	1,862
July	1,750	1,989	1,865
August	1,752	1,852	1,788
September	1,822	1,818	1,955
October	2,040	1,897	1,764
November	1,851	1,047	1,055
December	1,852	1,760	1,763

Apply adaptive filtering to the data in problem 1. Which forecasting method is easiest to use. Which gives the most accurate forecasts?

2. Following are midquarter prices for #2 hard winter wheat.

QUARTER

Year	I	II	III	IV
1970	1.53	1.53	1.54	1.63
1971	1.65	1.62	1.56	1.60
1972	1.61	1.64	1.86	2.29
1973	2.48	2.64	4.71	4.78
1974	5.78	3.67	4.36	4.99
1975	4.02	3.45	4.31	3.92
1976	4.08	3.76	3.24	2.79

Use the data to prepare an adaptive filtering model.
Prepare a goodness-of-fit analysis.
Evaluate the results of the model by comparing forecast results to actual prices one quarter ahead for the period after 1976. (These prices are available in *Survey of Current Business.*)

ADAPTIVE FILTERING PROGRAM

This program develops the weights for adaptive filtering analysis and prepares the initial forecast. The weights are developed from a set of starting weights by making the number of passes specified by the user over a set of historical data on the item to be forecast. All of the starting weights can be set equal to $1/n$ (where n is the number of weights being used), or the user can make an initial estimate of the weights.

The program contains the data from Table 6–3. In order to use the program, it is only necessary to replace this data with your own. The first data set consists of the number of observations, the smoothing constant, the number of weights to be used, and the number of passes through the data to be used in training the weights. The second data set consists of the historical observations, from the oldest to the most recent.

```
10 DIM A(72)
20 READ N,K,V,C
30 FOR I = 1 TO V
40 READ A(N+I)
50 NEXT I
60 FOR I = 1 TO N
70 READ A(I)
```

```
 80 NEXT I
 90 PRINT "PASS        STANDARD ERROR"
100 FOR L = 1 TO C
110 LET S = 0
120 FOR I = V+1 TO N
130 LET F = 0
140 LET Y = 0
150 FOR J = 1 TO V
160 IF A(I-J) > Y THEN LET Y = A(I-J)
170 LET F = F + A(N+J)*A(I-J)
180 NEXT J
190 LET S = S + (A(I)-F)*(A(I)-F)
200 FOR J = 1 TO V
210 LET A(N+J) = A(N+J)+2*K*((A(I)-F)/(Y*Y))*A(I-J)
220 NEXT J
230 NEXT I
240 PRINT L, SQR(S/(N-V))
250 NEXT L
260 PRINT
270 PRINT "WEIGHTS (IN ORDER FROM T-1 THROUGH T-N)"
280 FOR J = 1 TO V
290 PRINT A(N+J),
300 NEXT J
800 DATA 12,.25,4,20
810 DATA .2,.2,.2,.4
820 DATA 10284,7601,11802,13533,10171,7941
830 DATA 11561,13779,11306,9307,11265,12531
999 END
```

Usage

The first statement in the program sets up space for analysis. This DIM statement must be set to equal at least the number of observations plus the number of weights to be used. Thus, the present dimension of 72 could handle 60 observations with 12 weights. The 72 can be replaced with a larger number if a larger forecasting problem is being analyzed.

You may want to enter data from a file rather than from DATA statements in this program. This can be achieved by replacing the READ statements with your computer's file read instruction. The data can be entered from the keyboard during execution by eliminating the DATA statements and replacing statements 20 through 70 with the following.

```
20 PRINT "HOW MANY OBSERVATIONS?"
21 INPUT N
22 PRINT "WHAT IS THE SMOOTHING CONSTANT?"
23 INPUT K
24 PRINT "HOW MANY WEIGHTS?"
25 INPUT V
26 PRINT "HOW MANY TRAINING PASSES?"
```

```
27 INPUT C
28 PRINT "ENTER THE STARTING WEIGHTS IN ORDER FROM T-1"
29 PRINT "     THROUGH T-N, ONE WEIGHT PER LINE"
30 FOR I = 1 TO V
40 INPUT A(N+I)
50 NEXT I
55 PRINT "ENTER THE OBSERVATIONS IN ORDER FROM OLDEST TO"
56 PRINT "     MOST RECENT, ONE OBSERVATION PER LINE"
60 FOR I = 1 TO N
70 INPUT A(I)
```

This program is designed to perform the time–consuming project of developing initial weights. When the forecasts are to be repeated on a regular basis, such as weekly or monthly, a short, simple program is needed for the updating and preparation of each new forecast. The following short program could be used for updating and for new forecast preparation.

```
10 DIM A(30)
20 PRINT "HOW MANY WEIGHTS"
30 INPUT N
40 PRINT "ENTER THE WEIGHTS IN ORDER FROM T-1 THROUGH T-N"
50 FOR I = 1 TO N
60 INPUT A(N+I+1)
70 NEXT I
80 PRINT "WHAT IS THE TRAINING CONSTANT?"
90 INPUT K
100 PRINT "ENTER THE ";N+1;" OBSERVATIONS IN ORDER"
110 PRINT "     FROM T THROUGH T-N"
120 INPUT A(1)
130 LET S = 0
140 FOR I = 2 TO N+1
150 INPUT A(I)
160 IF A(I)>S THEN LET S = A(I)
170 LET F = F + A(I)*A(N+I)
180 NEXT I
190 PRINT "PERIOD     OLD WEIGHT     NEW WEIGHT"
200 FOR I = 1 TO N
210 LET W = A(N+I+1) + 2*K*((A(1) - F)/(S*S))*A(I+1)
220 PRINT "T-";I,A(N+I+1),W
230 LET A(N+I+1) = W
240 LET P = P + A(N+I+1)*A(I)
250 NEXT I
260 PRINT
270 PRINT "THE NEW FORECAST IS ";P
280 END
```

7

EXPONENTIAL SMOOTHING

Like other time series projection techniques, exponential smoothing relies on past values of a series to forecast future values of that same series. This technique is particularly useful when repeated forecasts covering periods from a week to a few months are needed for a large number of items. Companies producing hundreds of products and needing regularly updated short-term forecasts of sales or costs for each product have found exponential smoothing to be ideal.

Like the techniques covered in Chapter 6, exponential smoothing uses a weighted average of past observations to reduce the impact of random movements and estimate patterns such as trends and seasonal variations. The weighting method used in exponential smoothing has the desirable property of placing proportionally more weight (emphasis) on recent observations while still including older observations in the analysis. Exponential smoothing allows the forecaster considerable flexibility in deciding the relative emphasis to be placed on recent versus older observations, thus improving his ability to identify patterns and forecast accurately.

Once an exponential smoothing model has been developed for a particular time series, it is extremely simple to update the model and prepare new forecasts each period. The amount of data that must be carried forward from period to period is extremely limited and the updating calculation is quick and easy. Yet, offsetting the ease of updating is the time required to first set up and then test an exponential smoothing model. While the updating of the forecast each period is so simple that the method has been used where computers were not available, numerous calculations are required to develop the model. The computer program at the end of the chapter can handle these computations quickly.

THREE EXPONENTIAL SMOOTHING APPLICATIONS

There are three forms of exponential smoothing that can be applied to forecasting problems. The simplest form of exponential smoothing is used when there is neither cyclical variation nor a trend in the series to be forecast.[1] Another form of exponential smoothing is used when there is a trend, and a third form is used when cyclical variations exist, with or without a trend. These three forms of exponential smoothing are explained in the remainder of this chapter.

Simple Exponential Smoothing

Refined glycerine production, represented by the solid line in Figure 7-1, is an example of a time series for which simple exponential smoothing could be used. The series contains neither a trend nor a cyclical pattern. Monthly production can be thought of as moving randomly around a value referred to as the *location* of the series. The location is unknown and must be estimated from past observations. Furthermore, the location may shift, either gradually or abruptly. Simple exponential smoothing computes a smoothed value of the time series with greater weight given to more recent observations. This serves to dampen the effects of random fluctuations while still allowing shifts in location to be recognized. The dashed line in Figure 7-1 is an example of a series of forecasts developed using simple exponential smoothing.

The exponentially smoothed value of a time series is computed using the formula

$$S_t = wY_t + (1-w)S_{t-1} \qquad (7\text{-}1)$$

where

Y_t = the value of a series for a particular period. If we are examining monthly sales beginning January, 1977, Y_7 would be actual sales for July, 1977.

---

[1]Graphical analysis or decomposition can be used to find out if there is a pattern.

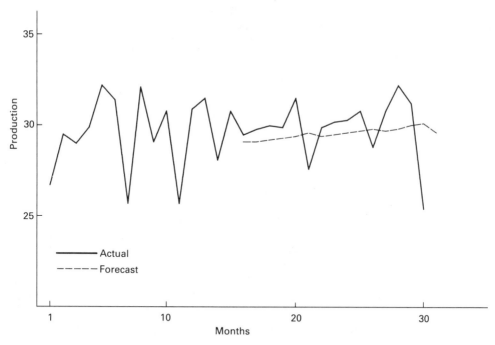

FIGURE 7-1 Refined Glycerine Production

S_{t-1} = the smoothed value of the time series as of period $t-1$. It is the current estimate of location after the actual value of Y was observed for period $t-1$.

S_t = the smoothed value of the series after the actual value of Y was observed for period t.

w = a weighting factor, between zero and one. The larger the w, the greater the emphasis placed on more recent observations. The selection of a proper w will be discussed later in this chapter.

The smoothed value for a period is a weighted average of the actual value for that period and the smoothed value for the previous period, which is in turn a weighted average of the actual value for the previous period and the smoothed value of the period before, etc. Thus, the smoothed value of a series for a particular period is a weighted average of all past observations.[2] The use of simple exponential smoothing can

[2] $S_t = wY_t + (1-w)S_{t-1}$ and $S_{t-1} = wY_{t-1} + (1-w)S_{t-2}$

Substituting,

$$S_t = wY_t + (1-w) [wY_{t-1} + (1-w)S_{t-2}]$$

$$= wY_t + w(1-w) Y_{t-1} + (1-w)^2 S_{t-2}$$

95

Table 7-1
EXPONENTIAL SMOOTHING OF EGG SALES

Week	Cases Sold	Smoothed Value
1	114	114
2	121	$S_2 = (0.2)121 + (1 - 0.2)114 = 115$
3	119	$S_3 = (0.2)119 + (1 - 0.2)115 = 116$
4	120	$S_4 = (0.2)120 + (1 - 0.2)116 = 117$

be demonstrated with a short time series. Weekly sales of eggs at Ward's Grocery Mart are shown in Table 7-1. Week 4 is the most recent week. The objective is to forecast sales for week 5 and set up a forecasting system that can be easily updated for each succeeding week.

The first step is to prepare a smoothed value or estimate of location for week 1. With only one observation, the smoothed value for week 1 is the same as the actual value—114. To compute a smoothed value for week 2, a value for w is needed. A w of 0.2 was chosen in this case, using methods to be discussed later. The smoothed value for week 2 is then computed as a weighted average of actual sales for week 2 and the smoothed value for week 1:

$$S_2 = wY_2 + (1-w)S_1 = (0.2)121 + (1-0.2)114 = 115$$

The process is then repeated for S_3 and S_4. Thus, the smoothed value for week 4 is effectively a weighted average of the actual sales for weeks 1 through 4. These computations are summarized in Table 7-1.

Since no trend is anticipated, the forecast for the next period, F_{t+1} is the latest estimate of location, S_t. Thus, the egg sales forecast for week 5 is

$$F_5 = S_4 = 117$$

Further updates are very simple. If actual sales for week 5 turned out to be 121, the smoothed value for week 5 would be

$$S_5 = (0.2)121 + (1-0.2)117 = 118$$

[2](*continued*)

This substitution can be continued indefinitely:

$$S_t = wY_t + w(1-w)Y_{t-1} + w(1-w)^2 Y_{t-2} + w(1-w)^3 Y_{t-3} + \ldots$$

Thus, S_t is a weighted average of all past values of the series.

and the forecast for week 6 would be the smoothed value for week 5—118.

Only three numbers are required to prepare the smoothed value for week 5: the w factor, the smoothed value for the previous week, and the actual sales for week 5. Once a simple exponential smoothing model has been set up, the forecast can be updated each period using only three numbers and one simple calculation. The modest effort required to set up the model is rewarded with a forecasting system that is extremely easy to update. Furthermore, the forecast is a weighted average of all past observations, since S_t is actually a weighted average of all past observations.

As was done with the egg sales forecast, it is necessary to initialize or warm-up the model with several periods of history so that the first actual forecast will be a weighted average of a series of past observations. As a rule of thumb, the minimum number of periods used to initialize the model would be at least

$$T = (2/w) - 1 \qquad (7\text{-}2)$$

Even if an infinite number of historical periods were available, more than 85 percent of the total weight would be assigned to the first $2/w - 1$ periods.

With a w of 0.2, we would have liked to use at least $2/0.2 - 1 = 9$ periods of history to initialize the model. Limited history frequently makes it necessary to prepare the first forecast based on a relatively few periods of history.[3]

The selection of a proper w is important. The higher the w, the greater the weight placed on more recent observations. The lower the

[3]For the more mathematically inclined, an alternative and preferable method for preparing the smoothed value with less than an ideal amount of history is

$$S_t = \frac{\sum_{t=0}^{T-1} (1-w)^t Y_{T-t}}{\sum_{t=0}^{T-1} (1-w)^t}$$

Using this method, the smoothed value for egg sales in period 4 would be

$$S_4 = \frac{120 + (0.8)119 + (0.8)^2 121 + (0.8)^3 114}{1 + (0.8) + (0.8)^2 + (0.8)^3} = \frac{351}{2.952} = 119$$

Forecasts and later smoothing would then be prepared in the normal manner. This method avoids the problem of overemphasizing the first value, Y_t, in a series with a short history.

w, the less forecasts will be affected by random movements. On the other hand, the lower the *w*, the slower the adjustment to shifts in location.

The *w* may be selected arbitrarily or, if sufficient data is available, may be chosen by testing several values to determine which provides the best forecasts. Table 7-2 shows the evaluation of several *w* values for monthly production of refined glycerine. The analysis is shown for *w* values of 0.1, 0.3, and 0.5. Weights in the lower part of the range from 0.0 to 1.0 were chosen because experience has shown that the optimal weights are generally found in that range. Since *w* values as small as 0.1 were tested, it would have been ideal to follow equation 7-2 and use $2/0.1 - 1 = 19$ periods to initialize the model. However, with only thirty months of history available, this would have left a limited time for testing the forecasts produced with alternate *w* values. As a compromise, fifteen months were used to initialize the model, and fifteen months were used to test alternate *w* values. The objective is to select the *w* which produces the smallest standard error.

In this test, the lowest standard error was found at $w = 0.1$. One might decide to continue the search for the best *w* in the neighborhood of 0.1, trying 0.05 and 0.15 or 0.2. However, experience has shown that the average error is not very sensitive to small changes in *w* close to the optimal value of *w*.[4] Using the *w* of 0.10, the smoothed value for month 30, and therefore the forecast for month 31, would be 29.6.

While some effort was expended in developing the model and preparing the first forecast, it takes only a few seconds to update the estimate of *S* and prepare a new forecast. Furthermore, if the company produces a whole class of similar products, the same *w* value will probably be used for all such products, again reducing the amount of effort required.

Exponential Smoothing with Trend Patterns

Many times series have a trend component; for example, sales may be gradually increasing or decreasing over time. The time series may then be thought of as a series of random movements and a trend line. The trend line is not known and must be estimated from the observations. Furthermore, the trend line may shift in either slope or location. The solid line in Figure 7-2 is an example of a time series with both trend and random movements. The dashed line is an example of a set of forecasts prepared using exponential smoothing. Exponential smoothing responds to shifts in location and trend while not being overly influenced by random movements.

[4]If we were to continue testing around 0.1 in increments as small as 0.005, the smallest standard error would be 1.700, found at $w = 0.125$.

Table 7-2
TESTING OF ALTERNATE W VALUES FOR REFINED GLYCERINE PRODUCTION

Month t	Production	$w = 0.1$			$w = 0.3$			$w = 0.5$		
		S_t	F_t	Error Squared	S_t	F_t	Error Squared	S_t	F_t	Error Squared
1	26.7	26.7			26.7			26.7		
2	29.5	27.0			27.5			28.1		
3	29.0	27.2			28.0			28.6		
4	29.9	27.5			28.6			29.3		
5	32.2	28.0			29.7			30.8		
6	31.4	28.3			30.2			31.1		
7	25.7	28.0			28.9			28.4		
8	32.1	28.4			29.9			30.3		
9	29.1	28.5			29.7			29.7		
10	30.8	28.7			30.0			30.3		
11	25.7	28.4			28.7			28.0		
12	30.9	28.7			29.4			29.5		
13	31.5	29.0			30.0			30.5		
14	28.1	28.9			29.4			29.3		
15	30.8	29.1			29.8			30.1		
16	29.5	29.1	29.1	0.16	29.7	29.8	0.09	29.8	30.1	0.36
17	29.8	29.2	29.1	0.49	29.7	29.7	0.01	29.8	29.8	0.00
18	30.0	29.3	29.2	0.64	29.8	29.7	0.09	29.9	29.8	0.04
19	29.9	29.4	29.3	0.36	29.8	29.8	0.01	29.9	29.9	0.00
20	31.5	29.6	29.4	4.41	30.3	29.8	2.89	30.7	29.9	2.56
21	27.6	29.4	29.6	4.00	29.5	30.3	7.29	29.2	30.7	9.61
22	29.9	29.5	29.4	0.25	29.6	29.5	0.16	29.6	29.2	0.49
23	30.2	29.6	29.5	0.49	29.8	29.6	0.36	29.9	29.6	0.36
24	30.3	29.7	29.6	0.49	30.0	29.8	0.25	30.1	29.9	0.16
25	30.8	29.8	29.7	1.21	30.2	30.0	0.64	30.5	30.1	0.49
26	28.8	29.7	29.8	1.00	29.8	30.2	1.96	29.7	30.5	2.89
27	30.8	29.8	29.7	1.21	30.1	29.8	1.00	30.3	29.7	1.21
28	32.2	30.0	29.8	5.76	30.7	30.1	4.41	31.3	30.3	3.61
29	31.2	30.1	30.0	1.44	30.9	30.7	0.25	31.3	31.3	0.01
30	25.4	29.6	30.1	22.09	29.3	30.9	30.25	28.4	31.3	34.81
Total Squared Error				44.00			49.66			56.60
Standard Error				1.713			1.820			1.943

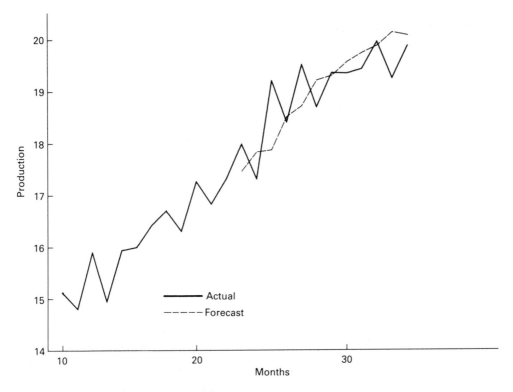

FIGURE 7-2 Nitrogen Gas Production

Either an additive (linear) or a percentage–growth (ratio) pattern can be used. Selection of the wrong trend model is seldom a serious problem due to the short-term nature of the forecasts and the fact that both trend and location are reestimated each period. A pattern of decline rather than growth presents no particular problem. A decline is simply negative growth, representing a unit or percentage decline each period.

With simple exponential smoothing, a smoothed estimate of location was developed. In the present case, smoothed estimates of both location (S_t) and trend (R_t) are developed. A new weighting factor, q, is used for estimation of trend. Like w, q takes a value between 0 and 1. The smoothed estimates of location and linear trend are computed using the following formulas:

$$S_t = w_t Y_t + (1-w)(S_{t-1} + R_{t-1}) \tag{7-3}$$

$$R_t = q(S_t - S_{t-1}) + (1-q)R_{t-1} \tag{7-4}$$

Table 7-3
EXPONENTIAL SMOOTHING OF CIGARETTE SALES

Week	Sales[*] Y_t	Location[*] S_t	Trend[**] R_t
1	5,000	5,000	50
2	5,080	5,056	52
3	5,120	5,110	53
4	5,150	5,160	52

[*]$w = 0.2$
[**]$q = 0.3$

The forecast for the next period (F_{t+1}) is based on this period's estimates of location and trend.[5]

$$F_{t+1} = S_t + R_t \qquad (7\text{-}5)$$

As with simple exponential smoothing, the forecasting model is extremely easy to update, but requires some effort to set up in the first place. The technique is illustrated with weekly sales of cigarettes at Franklin Drug Store (see Table 7-3). Sales for the last four weeks, along with an exponential smoothing analysis, are shown. Weights of $w = 0.2$ and $q = 0.3$ are used in this case. To begin the smoothing, initial estimates of S and R are needed. We let S_1 be the first value of Y: 5,000. R_1 is the average increase per period over the periods to be used for initializing the model:

$$R_1 = (Y_T - Y_1)/(T - 1) \qquad (7\text{-}6)$$

where T is the number of periods to be used for initialization. In this case, $R_1 = (5{,}150 - 5{,}000)/3 = 50$. The first actual smoothing calculations then begin with period 2:

$$S_2 = (0.2)5{,}080 + (1-0.2)(5{,}000 + 50) = 5{,}056$$
$$R_2 = 0.3(5{,}056 - 5{,}000) + (1-0.3)50 = 52$$

---

[5]These formulas are for a linear or additive trend. For a percentage growth trend, the following formulas should be substituted.

$$S_t = wY_t + (1-w)(S_{t-1}R_{t-1})$$
$$R = q(S_t/S_{t-1}) + (1-q)R_{t-1}$$
$$F_{t+1} = S_tR_t$$

The procedure is then repeated for periods 3 and 4 (see Table 7-3).

With the initialization completed, the forecast for week 5 can be prepared. S_4 and R_4 are, respectively, the estimates of location and trend. Using equation 7-5, the forecast for week 5 is

$$F_5 = 5,160 + 52 = 5,212$$

If one wishes to forecast k periods into the future, the forecasting formula is[6]

$$F_{t+k} = S_t + kR_t \qquad (7\text{-}7)$$

For example, if Franklin Drug Store wishes to forecast cigarette sales four weeks into the future, the forecast would be

$$F_8 = 5,160 + 4(52) = 5,368$$

Updating is again a simple procedure. It is only necessary to apply equations 7-3, 7-4, and 7-5 each period to update the S and R estimates and prepare a new forecast.

While the example used only four weeks of history, one would typically prefer at least $2/w - 1$ periods to initialize the model. In this case, $2/0.2 - 1 = 9$ periods of history would have been preferred to initialize the model before forecasting.

The selection of proper weights for smoothing is more time consuming than for simple exponential smoothing since w and q weights must be tested *in combination*. Production of nitrogen gas is used to illustrate the selection of weights (see Figure 7-2). Since weights as small as $w = 0.0$ were tested, a very large number of periods would be ideal for initializing the model. However, only twenty-four periods of history are available and some periods are needed for testing alternate weights. Thus, twelve months of history were used to initialize the model and twelve months were used to evaluate forecasts prepared with alternate weights. The calculations for $w = 0.3$ and $q = 0.1$ are shown in Table 7-4.

Analysis like that shown in Table 7-4 was performed for various combinations of w and q values. The results are shown in Table 7-5. Of the weights checked in the table, $w = 0.3$ and $q = 0$ produce the lowest

---

[6]For a percentage growth model, the formula is

$$F_{t+k} = S_t R_t^k$$

Table 7-4
EXPONENTIAL SMOOTHING OF NITROGEN GAS PRODUCTION

Month	Production Y_t	Location[a] S_t	Trend[b] R_t	Forecast F_t	Error Squared
1	15,118	15,118[c]	200[d]		
2	14,804	15,164	185		
3	15,899	15,514	202		
4	14,946	15,485	179		
5	15,936	15,746	187		
6	15,994	15,951	189		
7	16,411	16,221	197		
8	16,697	16,502	205		
9	16,302	16,586	193		
10	17,260	16,923	207		
11	16,827	17,039	198		
12	17,316	17,261	200		
13	17,982	17,617	216	17,461	271,441
14	17,307	17,675	200	17,833	276,676
15	19,205	18,274	240	17,875	1,768,900
16	18,404	18,481	237	18,514	12,100
17	19,512	18,956	261	18,718	630,436
18	18,691	19,059	245	19,217	276,676
19	19,354	19,319	247	19,304	2,500
20	19,344	19,499	240	19,566	49,284
21	19,425	19,645	231	19,739	98,596
22	19,950	19,898	233	19,876	5,476
23	19,243	19,865	206	20,131	788,544
24	19,862	20,008	200	20,071	43,681

Total Squared Error   4,224,310
Standard Error   593

[a] $w = 0.3$ [c] $S_1 = Y_1 = 15,118$
[b] $q = 0.1$ [d] $R_1 = (Y_{12} - Y_1)/(12-1) = (17,316 - 15,118)/11 = 200$

standard error: 574.[7] Using the location and trend estimates computed with these weights in Table 7-5, the forecast for period 25 is

$$F_{25} = 19,945 + 200 = 20,145$$

[7] If we were to test weights from 0 to 0.5 in increments of 0.05 in searching for the optimal weights, we find that $w = 0.25$ and $q = 0$ reduces the standard error slightly to 572. Extensive searching using ever smaller increments seldom results in substantial improvements in accuracy.

Table 7-5
STANDARD ERRORS WITH SELECTED COMBINATIONS OF W AND Q
FOR NITROGEN GAS PRODUCTION

W	Q	Standard Error	S_{24}	R_{24}
0.0	0.0	629	19,718	200
0.1	0.0	586	19,959	200
	0.1	600	20,088	221
	0.3	632	20,324	227
	0.5	664	20,437	181
0.3	0.0	574	19,945	200
	0.1	593	20,008	200
	0.3	605	19,960	114

As with simple exponential smoothing, the effort involved in initializing the model and testing alternate weights is rewarded with a forecasting system that is easy to update for each period. If production for period 25 turned out to be 20,000, the updating calculations would be

$$S_{25} = (0.3)20,000 + (1 - 0.3)20,145 = 20,102$$

$$R_{25} = (0)(20,102 - 20,000) + (1-0)200 = 200$$

$$F_{26} = 20,102 + 200 = 20,302$$

Only four numbers need to be carried over from the previous period: S_{t-1}, R_{t-1}, w, and q. Since the same weights are frequently used for a whole class of items, only two numbers—S_{t-1} and R_{t-1}—need to be stored and carried forward for each item.

Exponential Smoothing with Cyclical Patterns

In addition to random movements and trends, many time series follow a cyclical pattern, with what is called the annual or seasonal pattern being the most common. While the following example uses a seasonal pattern, the same approach can be used for cycles of any length.

Figure 7-3 is an example of a time series with a definite seasonal and a small trend pattern. A good forecasting technique should not only estimate the present location, trend, and seasonal pattern, but also should respond to shifts in any or all of these while limiting the response to random movements. In a manner analogous to that used when there was only a trend component, exponential smoothing can be used to provide smoothed estimates of location, trend, and seasonal patterns. The dashed line in Figure 7-3 represents a series of forecasts prepared with exponential smoothing.

Just as a trend can be either additive or percentage growth, a seasonal pattern can be either additive or ratio. The linear trend and ratio seasonal pattern are most widely used for exponential smoothing. The basic formulas for the linear trend and ratio seasonal pattern are:[8]

$$S_t = w(Y_t/P_{t-L}) + (1-w)(S_{t-1} + R_{t-1}) \qquad (7\text{-}8)$$

$$R_t = q(S_t - S_{t-1}) + (1-q)R_{t-1} \qquad (7\text{-}9)$$

$$P_t = z(Y_t/S_t) + (1-z)P_{t-L} \qquad (7\text{-}10)$$

where

w, q, and z are the weighting factors for estimation of location, trend, and seasonal pattern, respectively;

S_t, R_t, and P_t are the smoothed estimates of location, trend, and cyclical pattern, respectively;

Y_t is the actual value of the series in period t;

L is the number of periods per cycle; if monthly data is being used and there is a seasonal pattern, $L = 12$.

The formula for S_t, the location estimate, is the same as that used in the case of linear trend with the exception that the most recent observation, Y_t, is divided by the cyclical factor estimate developed at

---

[8]For an additive trend and additive seasonal pattern, equations 7-8 and 7-10 would be replaced by

$$S_t = w (Y_t - P_{t-L}) + (1-w)(S_{t-1} + R_{t-1})$$
$$P_t = z(Y_t - S_t) + (1-z)P_{t-L}$$

For a percentage growth and ratio seasonal pattern, equations 7-8 and 7-9 would be replaced by

$$S_t = w (Y_t/P_{t-L}) + (1-w)(S_{t-1}R_{t-1})$$
$$R_t = Q(S_t/S_{t-1}) + (1-q)R_{t-1}$$

For a percentage growth trend and additive seasonal pattern, equations 7-8, 7-9, and 7-10 would be replaced by

$$S_t = w (Y_t - P_{t-L}) + (1-w)(S_{t-1}R_{t-1})$$
$$R_t = q (S_t/S_{t-1}) + (1-q)R_{t-1}$$
$$P_t = z (Y_t - S_t) + (1-z)P_{t-L}$$

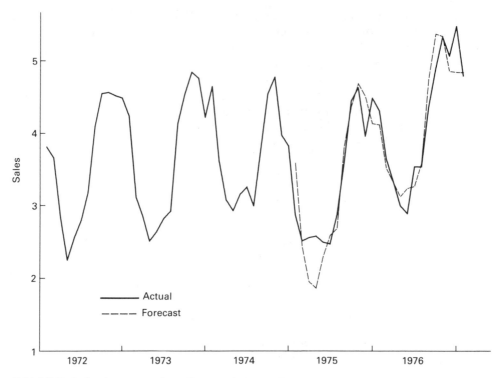

FIGURE 7-3 Replacement Auto Battery Sales (millions)

the same point in the previous cycle. The formula for R_t, the trend component, is the same as that previously used, and only the formula for P_t, the cyclical pattern, is new.

The use of the model is illustrated in Table 7-6 using monthly sales of replacement auto batteries shown in Figure 7-3. Sales for 1972 through 1974 are used to initialize the model. Development of the beginning estimates—S_0, R_0, P_0, P_{-1}, . . . , P_{-11}—will be discussed after the basic technique is illustrated.

Using formulas 7-8, 7-9, and 7-10, and w, q, and z of 0.3, 0.5, and 0.3 respectively, the estimates for the first two months of 1972 are

$$S_1 = 0.3(3,804/1.177) + (1 - 0.3)(3,550 + 5) = 3,458$$

$$R_1 = 0.5(3,458 - 3,550) + (1 - 0.5)5 = -43$$

$$P_1 = 0.3(3,804/3,458) + (1 - 0.3)1.177 = 1.154$$

$$S_2 = 0.3(3,654/.894) + (1 - 0.3)(3,458 - 43) = 3,617$$

$$R_2 = 0.5(3,617 - 3,458) + (1 - 0.5)(-43) = 58$$

$$P_2 = 0.3(3,654/3,617) + (1 - 0.3).894 = 0.929$$

The procedure is repeated for each period to produce the results shown in Table 7-6.

The forecasting formula is

$$F_{t+1} = (S_t + R_t)P_{t-L+1} \qquad (7\text{-}11)$$

For example, the battery sales forecast for month 37 is

$$F_{37} = (S_{36} + F_{36})P_{25} = (3{,}215 - 125)1.157 = 3{,}575$$

If one wishes to forecast more than one period into the future, the forecasting formula is

$$F_{t+k} = (S_t + kR_t)P_{t-L+k} \qquad (7\text{-}12)$$

where k is the number of periods into the future we wish to forecast.[9] For example, the period 40 forecast, based on observations through period 36, would be

$$F_{40} = [3{,}215 + 4(-125)] \, 0.701 = 1{,}903$$

The development of beginning estimates of S, R, and P factors is somewhat more difficult when cyclical factors are present because the cyclical pattern for a particular period is only reevaluated once each cycle. Using three years of monthly data, for example, there will be thirty-six opportunities to reevaluate the R and S estimates, but only three opportunities to reevaluate the seasonal factor for each month.

The preferred approach to developing beginning estimates is to perform a simple decomposition analysis (Chapter 5) of the data to be used for initializing the model. The decomposition analysis yields the location, cyclical pattern, and trend estimates. Table 5-1 in Chapter 5 shows a simple decomposition analysis of the same battery sales data used as an exponential smoothing illustration in this chapter. The

---

[9]For an additive trend and additive cyclical pattern, the forecasting formula is

$$F_{t+k} = S_t + kR_t + P_{t-L+k}$$

For a percentage growth trend and ratio cyclical factor, the forecasting formula is

$$F_{t+k} = (S_t R_t^k)P_{t-L+k}$$

For a percentage growth trend and an additive cyclical factor, the forecasting formula is

$$F_{t+k} = S_t R_t^k + P_{t-L+k}$$

Table 7-6
EXPONENTIAL SMOOTHING WITH TREND AND CYCLICAL PATTERNS

Refer-ence	t	Series Y	Smoothed Value S ($w=0.3$)	Trend R ($q=0.5$)	Cyclical Factor P ($z=0.3$)	Forecast F	Error^2 $(Y-F)^2$
	−11				1.177		
	−10				0.894		
	−9				0.789		
	−8				0.723		
	−7				0.771		
	−6				0.814		
	−5				0.831		
	−4				1.114		
	−3				1.228		
	−2				1.265		
	−1				1.238		
	0		3550	5	1.157		
72-1	1	3804	3458	−43	1.154		
2	2	3654	3617	58	0.929		
3	3	2826	3647	44	0.785		
4	4	2249	3517	−43	0.698		
5	5	2558	3427	−66	0.764		
6	6	2794	3382	−55	0.818		
7	7	3178	3476	20	0.856		
8	8	4086	3548	46	1.125		
9	9	4538	3624	61	1.235		
10	10	4553	3659	48	1.259		
11	11	4507	3687	38	1.233		
12	12	4473	3767	59	1.166		
73-1	13	4226	3777	35	1.143		
2	14	3108	3672	−35	0.904		
3	15	2837	3630	−38	0.784		
4	16	2503	3590	−39	0.698		
5	17	2631	3519	−55	0.759		
6	18	2807	3454	−60	0.816		
7	19	2915	3397	−58	0.857		
8	20	4120	3436	−9	1.147		
9	21	4526	3498	27	1.253		
10	22	4830	3618	74	1.282		
11	23	4741	3738	97	1.244		
12	24	4208	3767	63	1.151		
74-1	25	4629	3896	96	1.157		

Table 7-6 *(continued)*

Refer-ence	t	Series Y	Smoothed Value S ($w = 0.3$)	Trend R ($q = 0.5$)	Cyclical Factor P ($z = 0.3$)	Forecast F	Error² $(Y-F)^2$
2	26	3607	3991	96	0.904		
3	27	3070	4036	71	0.777		
4	28	2920	4130	83	0.701		
5	29	3143	4191	72	0.756		
6	30	3244	4177	29	0.804		
7	31	2987	3990	−79	0.824		
8	32	3754	3720	−174	1.106		
9	33	4524	3565	−164	1.258		
10	34	4760	3495	−117	1.306		
11	35	3960	3320	−146	1.229		
12	36	3811	3215	−125	1.161		
75-1	37	2868	2907	−216	1.106	3575	499,849
2	38	2504	2715	−204	0.909	2433	5,041
3	39	2550	2742	−88	0.823	1951	358,801
4	40	2570	2958	64	0.751	1860	504,100
5	41	2487	3102	104	0.770	2285	40,804
6	42	2463	3163	83	0.796	2578	13,225
7	43	2865	3315	118	0.836	2675	36,100
8	44	3573	3372	88	1.092	3797	50,176
9	45	4432	3479	98	1.263	4353	6,241
10	46	4613	3564	92	1.302	4672	3,481
11	47	3948	3523	26	1.196	4493	297,025
12	48	4469	3639	71	1.181	4120	121,801
76-1	49	4294	3762	97	1.117	4103	36,481
2	50	3637	3902	119	0.916	3508	16,641
3	51	3321	4025	121	0.824	3309	144
4	52	2990	4097	97	0.745	3114	15,376
5	53	2882	4059	30	0.752	3229	120,409
6	54	3524	4190	81	0.810	3255	72,361
7	55	3523	4254	73	0.834	3571	2,304
8	56	4335	4220	20	1.073	4725	152,100
9	57	4872	4125	−37	1.238	5355	233,289
10	58	5313	4086	−38	1.301	5323	100
11	59	5052	4101	−11	1.207	4841	44,521
12	60	5460	4250	69	1.212	4830	396,900

Sum = 3,027,270

Standard Error = $\sqrt{3,027,270/24}$ = 355

beginning estimates for P_{-11} through P_0 are the cyclical factor estimates from the simple decomposition. The trend and location estimates, R_0 and S_0 are the trend estimate, b, and the intercept value, a, from the simple decomposition. Using this approach for the development of smoothing estimates, three cycles of data are normally sufficient to develop preforecasting estimates.

Shortcut procedures are sometimes used if many periods of data are available for initializing the model. For example, the seasonal factors can all be set at 1.0, R can be set at 0.0, and S can be set equal to the observed value of the series for the first period. If the number of periods of data available for initializing the model is large enough, the poor beginning estimates will eventually be overcome.

The selection of w, q, and z weights is again done by trial and error. The selection of proper weights can be quite time consuming in this case since weights must be examined in combination. Table 7-6 shows an evaluation of the weights $w = 0.3$, $q = 0.5$, and $z = 0.3$ for automobile replacement battery sales using two years of test data.

Table 7-7 shows standard error figures for various combinations of w, q, and z. The minimum standard error of 355 is found at $w = 0.3$, $q = 0.5$, and $z = 0.3$.

To prepare Table 7-7, it was necessary to repeat the analysis of Table 7-6 twenty-seven times. Fortunately, this can be done in fifteen minutes or so using the program at the end of this chapter.

Once the optimal set of weights is identified, forecasting can begin. Suppose, for example, that forecasts are desired for the first three months of 1977, based on data through the end of 1976. Using

Table 7-7
STANDARD ERRORS FOR AUTO REPLACEMENT BATTERY SALES FORECASTS

w	q	z 0.1	z 0.3	z 0.5
0.1	0.1	531	538	560
	0.3	591	621	673
	0.5	674	718	783
0.3	0.1	401	395	397
	0.3	383	367	362
	0.5	367	355	363
0.5	0.1	370	358	356
	0.3	370	358	361
	0.5	384	376	389

formula 7-12, the forecast for each of the first three months of 1977 would be

$$F_{61} = [4,250 + 69]1.117 = 4,824$$

$$F_{62} = [4,250 + 2(69)]\ 0.916 = 4,019$$

$$F_{63} = [4,250 + 3(69)]\ 0.824 = 3,673$$

As each additional month's actual data becomes known, the model can be updated with formulas 7-8, 7-9, and 7-10; and the forecasts can be updated.

Applications of Exponential Smoothing

The strength of exponential smoothing lies in good short-term accuracy combined with quick, low-cost updating. The technique has been widely used when regularly monthly or weekly forecasts were needed for a large number of items.

When compared to other time series methods, the primary disadvantage of this technique is the start-up time required. For this reason, the technique is seldom used when only a one-time forecast is desired. A second problem is that the forecaster must have an idea of the type of cyclical pattern involved, if any. The technique will not seek out an unsuspected cyclical pattern, as adaptive filtering will some-times do. This problem is not normally severe as strong cyclical patterns are generally known to the forecaster or can be identified through simple graphical analysis. The most significant weakness of this technique is one shared by all time series techniques: no outside variables are considered. Shifts in patterns are recognized only after they occur; turning points, other than cyclical ones, are never recognized in advance. To overcome this problem, many successful applications of exponential smoothing allow for some method of including other information which may affect the forecasts. The most common approach is to give a knowledgeable person responsibility for making adjustments with regard to other information. Thus, a successful system generally combines exponential smoothing fore-casts with human judgment.

Human judgment can be entered into the model in one of several ways. A one-time change in Y_t, such as a special order that is not likely to be repeated, can be handled by simply subtracting that amount from Y_t before performing the updating calculations. Known shifts in S, R, or P, which might occur for reasons such as acquisition of a major new customer, can be handled by direct adjustment to these values. Knowledge of approaching changes can also be recognized through direct adjustment of the forecasts. The latter type of adjustment is probably the most common.

Finally, as with any forecasting system, continued monitoring is required, using the techniques discussed in Chapter 10. Average error figures should continually be reevaluated, and special attention should be given to large errors with the goal of finding out what caused such errors and avoiding them in the future. In addition, the smoothing weights should be reexamined periodically; those which were optimal at one time may not be optimal forever.

RELATED TECHNIQUES AND SUGGESTIONS FOR FURTHER READING

The exponential smoothing techniques used when trend and cyclical patterns are involved were developed by Peter Winters (see references, p. 113). Those interested in the theoretical development of the model will find useful either Winters' original article (1960) or a more advanced book by Montgomery and Johnson (1962) or by Brown (1962).

Closely related to exponential smoothing with trend only is the method of double exponential smoothing. While the location estimate for each period (S_t) used in simple exponential smoothing is effectively a weighted average of past observations, double exponential smoothing uses a weighted average of the weighted averages for past periods. Though higher forms such as triple exponential smoothing are possible, they are seldom used. The results obtained with double exponential smoothing are similar to those obtained using the exponential smoothing method with trend patterns discussed here. A technical discussion of double exponential smoothing is provided by Montgomery and Johnson (1962).

Both simple decomposition and moving average analysis, discussed in this book, are techniques that can be considered as alternatives to exponential smoothing. See Chapters 5 and 6 for discussions of the merits of those techniques.

The X–11 method, a decomposition technique developed by the U.S. Census Bureau, provides another alternative. McGlaughlin (1962) provides a good explanation of the X–11 method. This method is considerably more expensive to use than exponential smoothing and would not generally be used when repeated forecasts for a large number of items are desired.

The Box-Jenkins technique (1976) is an alternative when conditions necessary for its use are met. To use the Box-Jenkins technique, it is not necessary to know what kinds of patterns are in the data beforehand. Furthermore, the Box-Jenkins technique can successfully handle combinations of patterns beyond those that can be handled with other techniques. However, it is also the most expensive because it requires an expensive computer program and more sophisticated computer hardware than that needed for the other techniques discussed in this chapter. In addition, this technique is more difficult to learn, and thus has a higher cost in terms of the forecaster's time. More time is also required to analyze a time series with the Box-Jenkins method than with a method such as exponential smoothing. The Box-Jenkins method is not considered an alternative in situations in which large numbers of forecasts must be prepared each period. In addition to cost limitations, the method requires fifty and preferably one hundred periods of history for development of the model, and requires that patterns be relatively stable over that period. These data requirements limit its use in many situations. A good layman's discussion is presented by Wheelwright and Makridakis (1977), while the creators of the technique, Box and Jenkins (1976), present a more detailed and mathematically rigorous discussion.

REFERENCES

Box, George E. and Gwilym M. Jenkins. *Time Series Analysis.* 2nd. ed. San Francisco: Holden-Day, 1976.

Brown, Robert G. *Smoothing, Forecasting and Prediction of Discrete Time Series.* Englewood Cliffs, N.J.: Prentice-Hall, 1962.

McGlaughlin, R. L. "Time Series Forecasting." Marketing Research Technique Series No. 6. American Marketing Association, 1962.

Montgomery, Douglas C. and Lynwood A. Johnson. *Forecasting and Time Series Analysis.* New York, McGraw-Hill, 1962.

Wheelwright, Steven C. and Spyros Makridakis. *Forecasting Methods for Management.* New York: John Wiley, 1977.

Winters, Peter R. "Forecasting Sales by Exponentially Weighted Moving Averages." *Management Science* (April, 1960), pp. 324–342.

PROBLEMS

Suburban Appliance Center wants to use an exponential smoothing model for inventory control. Because of lead times for orders, forecasts must be made for two months ahead. Monthly sales of washers appear below.

	1980	1981	1982	1983
January	351	413	457	408
February	329	382	417	401
March	370	425	465	455
April	304	374	428	463
May	305	409	476	479
June	399	409	463	440
July	399	407	433	466
August	424	505	544	475
September	495	467	502	475
October	446	497	580	455
November	420	439	421	250
December	366	382	317	186

1. Develop an appropriate exponential smoothing model.

2. Evaluate the model with regard to accuracy.

3. Could the same set of weights be used to forecast dryer sales? television sales?

   Purity Chemicals is interested in setting up an exponential smoothing model to forecast monthly sales of individual products. For production planning purposes, it is necessary to forecast sales three months in advance. Following are monthly sales of one of the products, sodium trypolyphosphate, in tons. There is no seasonal pattern in sales.

	1981	1982	1983
January	83	89	69
February	87	79	69
March	84	87	76
April	86	81	73
May	94	85	69
June	95	83	78
July	95	83	78
August	88	80	83
September	82	74	84
October	83	75	87
November	75	75	87
December	75	76	82

1. Develop an appropriate exponential smoothing model.

2. Evaluate the model with regard to accuracy.

3. Comment on the appropriateness of this type of model for the forecasting problem at hand.

    Following are sales for Ohio Specialties. While no trend or seasonal pattern is evident, there appear to be major shifts caused by changes in economic conditions. The company has been using a simple exponential smoothing model with a *w* of 0.8 for short-term sales forecasts.

Month	Actual	Forecast	Month	Actual	Forecast
1	2,100	2,000	13	3,328	2,720
2	2,226	2,080	14	3,307	3,206
3	2,090	2,109	15	3,309	3,287
4	2,081	2,094	16	3,432	3,305
5	2,064	2,084	17	3,394	3,407
6	2,088	2,068	18	3,387	3,397
7	2,106	2,084	19	2,709	3,389
8	2,077	2,102	20	2,656	2,845
9	2,685	2,082	21	2,662	2,694
10	2,665	2,564	22	2,750	2,668
11	2,667	2,645	23	2,748	2,734
12	2,734	2,663	24	2,660	2,745

1. Evaluate the accuracy of the simple exponential smoothing model.

2. Comment on the appropriateness of the simple exponential smoothing model for this type of forecasting problem.

3. Suggest another forecasting method that might be more appropriate.

EXPONENTIAL SMOOTHING PROGRAM

This program develops an exponential smoothing model by analyzing a series of observations. Once the model has been developed using this program, the forecasts and updating can be carried out by hand or by using a simple program such as the one discussed following the explanation of this model development program. This program can be used with or without a cyclical pattern and with or without a trend pattern.

The program contains the data from Table 7-6. To use the program, it is only necessary to replace this data with your own. The first data set contains the weights for *w*, *q*, *z* (in that order), and a number, either 0 or 1. If the only output you want from the program is the standard error, use 0. This is done while testing different combinations of *w*, *q*, and *z* to find the combination that produces the smallest standard error. Using 1 will cause the computer to print essentially the equivalent of Table 7-6. It is generally used after the optimal weights have been found. If there is no trend, *q* is set at 0. If there is no cyclical pattern, *z* is set equal to 0.

The second data set consists of the number of observations, the number of periods per cycle (1 if there is no cycle), a beginning smoothed value estimate, a beginning estimate of trend, and the number of periods to be used to run-in the model before checking for accuracy. If, for example, there are 60 observations and 36 are to be used to run-in the model, the standard error will be based on the last 24 observations.

The third data set consists of the initial cyclical component estimates. These can be skipped if there are no cyclical components, but the cyclical component estimates that are presently in the program as DATA statements 820 and 830 must be removed. The cyclical component estimates should be in order from most recent backward. If, for example, the observations begin with January and there is a twelve-month cycle, the first seasonal component estimate should be for December, the second should be for November, etc.

The fourth data set consists of the observations themselves, from oldest to most recent.

When you run the program asking for a full output of the results, a statement will appear on the screen asking how many lines you want printed at a time. This is done because the full output frequently consists of many more lines than can appear on the screen at one time. The output would pass faster than it could be read if there was not some method of stopping the printing so you could look at it. Simply answer this question by entering the number of lines that can appear on your screen at one time. If you have modified the program so that the output is printed on paper, either eliminate statements 25 and 26 from the program or answer the question with a number larger than the number of observations.

```
10 DIM A(72)
20 READ W,Q,Z,M
40 IF M=0 THEN 55
45 PRINT "HOW MANY LINES OF DATA DO YOU WANT PRINTED AT A
TIME?"
50 INPUT G
```

```
 55 READ N,C,S,R,P
 60 IF C=1 THEN 80
 65 FOR I = 1 TO C
 70 READ A(N+I)
 75 NEXT I
 80 IF C=1 THEN A(N+1) = 1
 90 L = N + C + 1
100 FOR I = 1 TO N
105 LET H=H+1
106 IF H>1 THEN 110
107 IF M>0 THEN PRINT "T        Y                S
R                  P "
110 L = L - 1
120 IF L=N THEN L=N+C
130 F=(S+R)*A(L)
140 READ A(I)
150 IF I>P THEN E=E+(F-A(I))*(F-A(I))
160 T=W*(A(I)/A(L))+(1-W)*(S+R)
170 R=Q*(T-S)+(1-Q)*R
180 S=T
190 A(L)=Z*A(I)/S+(1-Z)*A(L)
192 IF M=0 THEN 200
195 PRINT I;A(I),S,R,A(L)
196 IF H<G THEN 200
197 LET H=0
198 PRINT "HIT ENTER TO CONTINUE"
199 INPUT H
200 NEXT I
210 X=E/(N-P)
215 PRINT "SE = ";SQR(X)
800 DATA .3,.5,.3,1
810 DATA 60, 12, 3550, 5, 36
820 DATA 1.157,1.238,1.265,1.228,1.114,.831
830 DATA .814,.771,.723,.789,.894,1.177
840 DATA 3804,3654,2826,2249,2558,2794
850 DATA 3178,4086,4538,4553,4507,4473
860 DATA 4226,3108,2837,2503,2631,2807
870 DATA 2915,4120,4526,4830,4741,4208
880 DATA 4629,3607,3070,2920,3143,3244
890 DATA 2987,3754,4524,4760,3960,3811
910 DATA 2868,2504,2550,2570,2487,2463
920 DATA 2865,3573,4432,4613,3948,4469
930 DATA 4294,3637,3321,2990,2882,3524
940 DATA 3523,4335,4872,5313,5052,5460
999 END
```

Application

This program is generally used to develop an exponential smoothing model by testing a number of different combinations of weights. A new set of weights can be tested by simply changing DATA statement 300.

The testing of two weight combinations is illustrated below. The first statement, in which the exponential smoothing program is called, will depend on a particular computer's file name instructions and on the name you gave the program when you stored it.

```
>LOAD"EXPO"
READY
>800 DATA .5,.5,.5,0
>RUN
SE = 388.692
READY
>800 DATA .5,.5,.3,0
>RUN
SE = 375.853
READY
>
```

This process can be continued until the optimal set of weights is found. Then, the program is run again with the optimal set of weights and with the 0 replaced by a 1 to get a full output of the analysis.

You may want to run the program using data from a file rather than data stored in the program itself. This is done by replacing the READ statements with the file reading statements appropriate for your particular computer. Entering the data from the terminal during execution would not work very well for this program. Data can be extensive, and data entered during execution will be lost if the computer is turned off.

The first statement in the program—10 DIM A(72)—sets up space for the analysis. The number in parentheses must be at least twice the number of observations plus the number of periods per cycle (or plus 1 if there is no cyclical pattern). If the number of observations is large, the number in parentheses must be changed accordingly.

Once the exponential smoothing model has been developed, forecasts and further updating can be done with a simple program or even using a programmable calculator. Following is an example of a simple program for this purpose. The data statement in the program provides five pieces of information. The first number should be set at 1 if there is a trend pattern and at 0 if there is not. The second number should be set at 1 if there is a cyclical pattern and at zero if there is not. The third through fifth numbers are w, q, and z respectively. Values of 0 should be entered for z and q if there is no trend or cyclical pattern. The DATA statement can be set for a large number of items and the information for each individual item can be entered from the keyboard during execution.

```
10 READ K,L,W,Q,Z
20 PRINT "WHAT IS THE OLD LOCATION ESTIMATE?"
30 INPUT S
40 IF K=0 THEN 70
50 PRINT "WHAT IS THE OLD TREND ESTIMATE?"
60 INPUT R
70 LET P=1
80 IF L=0 THEN 110
90  PRINT "WHAT  IS  THE  CYCLICAL  FACTOR  ESTIMATE  TO  BE
UPDATED?"
100 INPUT P
110 PRINT "WHAT WAS THE ACTUAL OUTCOME"
120 INPUT Y
130 LET F = (S+R)*P
140 LET T = W*(Y/P) + (1-W)*(S+R)
150 LET R = Q*(T-S) + (1-Q)*R
160 LET S = T
170 LET P = Z*(Y/S) + (1-Z)*P
180 PRINT "NEW ESTIMATES"
190 PRINT "LOCATION     TREND     CYCLICAL"
200 PRINT S,R,P
210 PRINT "HOW MANY PERIODS FORWARD DO YOU WANT TO"
220 PRINT "    FORECAST?  (0 MEANS STOP)"
230 INPUT T
240 IF T = 0 THEN 999
243 IF L=1 THEN 250
245 LET P=1
247 GOTO 280
250 PRINT "WHAT IS THE CYCLICAL FACTOR FOR THE FORECAST"
260 PRINT "    PERIOD?"
270 INPUT P
280 LET F = (S + R*T)*P
290 PRINT "THE FORECAST IS ";F
300 GOTO 210
800 DATA 1,0,.3,.1,0
999 END
```

8

MODELING AND SIMULATION

The problems treated in the previous chapters involved a relationship between the item to be forecast and some other variable(s). The relationship was always expressed as a single equation such as

$$\text{Sales}_t = 1{,}000 + 123 \times \text{temperature}_t + 0.0178 \times \text{population}_t$$

or

$$\text{Sales}_t = 0.3 \times \text{sales}_{t-1} + 0.3 \times \text{sales}_{t-2} \times 0.4 \times \text{sales}_{t-3}$$

Each of these equations can quite accurately be called a model. It is a simplified representation of the relationship between sales and a factor or factors believed to affect sales. However, its single-equation nature limits its usefulness in certain cases.

The two approaches to modeling and simulation discussed in this chapter are geared toward those readers with access to electronic worksheet programs such as Visicalc® or SuperCalc™ and with knowledge of computer programming languages. Simulation models consist of numerous equations rather than a single equation and frequently incorporate probability distributions as well as point estimates.

The characteristics and uses of simulation models can be illustrated with a model relating corporate financial performance to sales and other factors:

$$\text{Sales}_t = 1.05 \times \text{sales}_{t-1}$$
$$\text{Variable costs}_t = 3{,}000 + 0.60 \times \text{sales}_t$$
$$\text{Fixed costs}_t = 10{,}000 + \text{fixed costs}_{t-1}$$
$$\text{Earnings before tax}_t = \text{sales}_t - \text{variable costs}_t - \text{fixed costs}_t$$
$$\text{Tax}_t = 0.46 \times \text{earnings before tax}_t$$
$$\text{Net income}_t = \text{earnings before tax}_t - \text{tax}_t$$

Once a model of this type is developed, it can be used to prepare a single forecast of financial performance, or it can be used to study the impacts of certain other factors on the financial performance of the company. This latter use might be for the purpose of developing a range of possible errors for the various aspects of financial performance, or it may be done as part of planning—the critical variables can be identified and planning can then focus on those variables.

The above model of corporate performance is a *deterministic model.* It could be written as a computer program and, when run, it would give one set of income statement figures. The impacts of various factors on income would be examined by changing the appropriate information and running the model again. For example, impacts of changes in the ratio of variable costs to sales could be examined by running the model several times with several different possible numbers replacing the 0.6 used in the original model.

A *probabilistic* model deals with uncertainty in a more direct way. Suppose, for example, that there is 0.5 probability that variable costs will be 60 percent of sales, a 0.25 probability that they will be 70 percent of sales, and a 0.25 probability that they will be 50 percent of sales. In addition, sales growth rates of 10 percent and 0 percent for next period are equally likely. A potential investor is interested in the expected net income and the range of possible net income levels.

Resist the observation that there are only six possible outcomes, and the probability of each outcome can be easily computed. The approach being developed can be used when there are hundreds of possible outcomes and computation of exact probabilities would be nearly impossible.

One way to examine the various possible sales growth and variable cost figures would be to construct two simple roulette wheels (see Figure 8-1). The wheel on the left is spun and a sales growth rate of 10 percent or 0 percent is chosen, depending on whether the wheel stops with the arrow in the 10 percent or 0 percent zone. The wheel on the right is then spun and a value for the variable cost ratio is selected in the same manner. These two numbers are inserted in the model to compute net income. The net income is recorded, both wheels are spun again, and a new net income is computed. This process is repeated

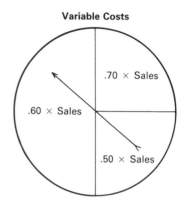

FIGURE 8-1 Monte Carlo Simulation

several hundred times, with the net income recorded each time. The resulting net incomes are then summarized with a frequency graph (bar chart) or by computing the mean and variance.

Even for this quite simple problem the process of spinning wheels and going through the computations would be quite time consuming. For a complex problem, it would simply be prohibitive. This is where the computer comes in. With the use of random number generators included as part of the BASIC language package in most personal computers, it is possible to have the computer carry out an activity that serves the same purpose as roulette wheel spinning. The computer can be instructed to carry out the operation a few hundred times and summarize the results in the form desired.

When uncertainty is directly included in the model in this manner, the model is referred to as a probabilistic model. The term Monte Carlo model is frequently used because of the analogy to spinning roulette wheels.

For those interested in terminology, *modeling* refers to the construction of a model. *Simulation* is the use of the model to predict outcomes, study the impacts of other factors, etc.

Although it might seem that the deterministic and probabilistic models are quite similar in concept, they are developed in substantially different ways. Deterministic models are generally used when a large number of relationships (equations) are involved and a number of different results must be considered. For example, financial planning models, which are extensions of the model used for illustration, are generally deterministic. Once the model is developed, the user performs sensitivity analysis, changing one factor or relationship at a time and examining the impact on a large number of financial performance measures. A Monte Carlo model, on the other hand, is more likely to be used when one or a few results are to be examined and a frequency distribution for a particular outcome is desired. Because of these differences, the two types of problem are treated in quite different ways. The deterministic models are generally developed using one of the electronic worksheet programs such as VisiCalc® or SuperCalc™. The probabilistic models are generally developed with the use of a computer programming language such as BASIC. The development of deterministic models is discussed first, followed by a discussion and illustration of Monte Carlo methods.

DETERMINISTIC MODELS

One wishing to construct deterministic models will most likely acquire one of the electronic worksheet programs that are available for most personal computers. While any model that can be developed using one of these programs could also be developed using BASIC programming language, the time savings are tremendous. The worksheet programs are also much easier to learn. The discussion of deterministic models is based on the assumption that you will be using one of these programs and will read the instructions that come with it.

The simple income statement used as an introduction to models on page 122 will be used for further discussion here. A financial statement is an appropriate example because the most common use of electronic worksheet programs is in the development of financial models. In fact, this use is so common that there are supplementary programs available to automatically set up the electronic worksheet for financial statement projection.

Model Development

A model may be ten or a hundred times as long as the example on page 122. But, like that simple model, it is merely a set of equations mathematically representing some activity. The construction of a model involves answering three questions:

1. What aspects of performance do I want to know about?
2. What factors are believed to affect those things identified in question one?
3. What are the precise relationships between the various factors identified in questions one and two?

In the simple example model, the aspect of performance that is of primary importance might be net income. When a financial model is used, it is expanded to report on other matters of interest—earnings per share, working capital needed, total assets needed, additional financing required, etc. The particular advantage of a model like this is that it allows the user to study many aspects of performance simultaneously.

Once the items of interest are identified, the next step is to determine what things affect the items of interest. The result is a sort of rough draft or nonspecific model. For the income statement example, a nonspecific model recognizing the various relationships might appear as follows.

$Sales_t = ?$

Variable costs$_t$ = some function of the sales level

Fixed costs = ?

Earnings before tax = sales − variable costs − fixed costs

Tax = some percentage of earnings before tax

Net income = earnings before tax − tax

This preliminary model consists of some vague and some specific statements. The statements that are specific at this point are *definitional.* One does not need to do any historical study to find out that net income equals earnings before tax minus tax.

In contrast, the vague statements address aspects of behavior, and are thus referred to as *behavioral* statements. The first behavioral statement is the sales level. Sales may be predicted using any of the forecasting methods studied in Chapters 2 through 7. The other aspects of behavior—variable costs, fixed costs, and taxes—might be made specific by studying the performance of the system in the past. For example, one might perform simple regression with variable costs as the dependent variable and sales as the independent variable. Simple regression coefficients of $a = 3,000$ and $b = 0.60$ would make it possible to convert this statement from vague to specific:

$$Variable\ costs_t = 3,000 + 0.60 \times sales_t$$

The other variables are studied in a similar manner. Apparently, the analyst in this case discovered that fixed costs increased each period, regardless of what happened to sales. A similar study of taxes results in specifying the average tax rate on income.

The process of moving from a nonspecific or rough draft model to a specific model is the most time-consuming and expensive part of the total model-building process. Observing that variable costs are related to sales requires minutes or seconds. Developing a precise estimate of the relationship between variable costs and sales may require hours or days. Regression analysis is widely used to move from general to specific relationships. Once the factors expected to affect a particular variable are identified, regression using historical data can provide an estimate of the relationship.

Once a model is developed, it is used to forecast and to examine the impacts of various changes in either company decisions or in the environment. Suppose 1983 sales were $7 million and we want to use the model to forecast financial results for 1984 through 1988. This could be done fairly easily with a simple calculator. Sales are simply assumed to increase 5 percent each year and fixed costs are assumed to increase by $10 thousand each year. The remaining items are determined in reference to the sales level using their equations. The five-year forecast appears in Table 8-1.

This model is, of course, extremely simple. A model would generally include balance sheet results as well as income statements, and a typical financial model might contain from thirty to fifty equations. Still, the set of forecasts in Table 8-1 can be performed with a calculator and paper nearly as easily as with a computer.

The advantages of the computer arise when the process is to be repeated. Suppose we want to know what would happen if sales increased at 4 percent instead of 5 percent, or if fixed costs increased at $11 thousand per year rather than $10 thousand. It would be necessary to set up a new table and repeat the entire series of calculations for each year for each of these changes. Any time the model is to be updated, the entire process must also be repeated.

This is where the computer comes in. With an electronic worksheet program, an entire new set of analysis can be had by changing one number. For example, one command will change the growth rate in sales as well as provide a complete new set of projected financial statements.

Table 8-1
FINANCIAL FORECAST

A	B	C	D	E	F	G
1	1983	1984	1985	1986	1987	1988
2 Sales	7000000	7350000	7717500	8103375	8508544	8933971
3 Variable costs	4203000	4413000	4633500	4865025	5108126	5363383
4 Fixed costs	2700000	2710000	2720000	2730000	2740000	2750000
5 Earn. bef. tax	97000	227000	364000	508350	660418	820588
6 Tax	44620	104420	167440	233841	303792	377471
7 Net income	52380	122580	196560	274509	356626	443117

An explanation of how to use an electronic worksheet program will not be attempted here. The specific instructions are unique for each particular program, and the programs come with complete instruction books. Instead, the discussion will be limited to a brief description of how these programs work.

An electronic worksheet program sets up a worksheet in the computer. As with a worksheet you might use on paper, each location on the worksheet can be identified by row and column. In Table 8-1, fixed costs for 1984 are located at column C and row 4 (the first row and first column in the table happen to be used for titles). When using an electronic worksheet program, the user simply tells the computer what he wants at each location. The choices are

1. A title, such as *Fixed Costs.*
2. A number, such as 1987 or 6732.58.
3. A formula.

It is the use of formulas to tell the computer what to put at a particular location that gives these programs their power. A common approach to notation identifies columns by letter and rows by number. Thus, the instruction to the computer with regard to variable costs in 1984 is

$$C3 = 3,000 + 0.60^*C2$$

where the asterisk (*) is used to indicate multiplication. A simple repeat instruction will tell the computer that you want D3, E3, F3, etc.— variable cost for each year—to be computed in the same way.

The electronic worksheet program completes all instructions as they are entered. Thus, by the time you have entered the last formula, you will have five years of income statements on the screen.

Now the power of these programs comes into play. You want to know what will happen if fixed costs increase at $11 thousand per year instead of $10 thousand. You simply retype one formula and almost instantly the financial statements for all five years will change accordingly. Although the advantages of such a program become visible with even this small model, they are much more obvious when the model becomes a bit larger. Suppose, for example, a company was preparing a monthly cash budget for the next year and there were two dozen different items of income and outflow. To see what would happen if there was a change in the pattern of accounts-receivable collections would require a minute or two to change one equation with the computer, and might require a couple of hours working on a paper worksheet with a pencil.

In developing and using models, simplicity and documentation should be kept in mind. The number of equations should be kept to the minimum needed to provide the information required. Excessive detail increases development cost, increases the risk of errors, and makes the results harder to use. Most model builders have observed an inverse relationship between complexity and usefulness.

If a model proves useful, simulation will normally be carried out over considerable time spans. Frequently, it will be necessary to modify the model as time goes by and as relationships change. Thus, it is important that each equation in the model be carefully documented so that it can be used and modified later. If you prepare a model today and want to use it again in a few months, a lack of documentation will probably force you to start over again.

Deterministic models, particularly with the aid of electronic worksheets, have proved useful in a number of settings. They have greatly reduced the time and expense required to predict the behavior of complex systems. More than this, they have made it possible to perform analysis that simply was not feasible in the past. One of their major benefits has been in bringing financial planning models to small businesses and even to individuals that could not have afforded them in the past.

PROBABILISTIC MODELS

In the case of deterministic models, uncertainty about some factor or relationship was handled by sensitivity analysis—trying several different values and studying what the changes did to the results. Probabilistic models handle uncertainty by allowing the user to enter a probability distribution for one or more variables and then to produce a probability distribution of results.

Probability models are generally used when only a few aspects of the results are of interest. Otherwise, the results become overwhelming; several dozen probability distributions of results are more information than most users can absorb. Probability distributions of any number of factors affecting results can be included. For example, probability distributions for a dozen items affecting sales and costs might be used to determine a single probability distribution of net income.

To develop a probability model, it is necessary to have a computer with a random number generator and to have knowledge of programming. The model developed here assumes a knowledge of BASIC programming language.

To develop the model, assume that a manager is trying to decide how much to hold in the bank balance and how much can be invested. The amount held in the bank balance must not only be sufficient to handle expected expenditures, but must also be a cushion to allow for uncertainty. For simplicity, we will treat only two components of cash flow: inflow and outflow. Neither inflow nor outflow are known with certainty, but both can be represented by probability distributions.

A probability distribution may be either continuous or discrete. A coin flip or the role of dice would involve discrete probability distributions. The coin can only provide whole numbers such as 1, 2, 3, etc. Temperature is an example of a continuous distribution. For any two temperatures you can give, there is always the possibility of a temperature between the two; between 20.278° and 20.279° there are an infinite number of possible temperatures, such as 20.2785°, 20.27857°, etc. If cash flows for the month could fall anywhere between $2 million and $50 million, the probability distribution over this range is nearly continuous. The only lack of continuity is caused by the fact that increments of less than a penny are not possible.

The computer can handle a discrete probability distribution easily and directly. Suppose that cash outflow per month is known to be $40,000, and there are only three possible levels of cash inflow for the month:

Cash Inflow	Probability
$ 20,000	0.25
50,000	0.60
100,000	0.15

Most computers have a random number generator that will generate a random number in the range from 0.0 to 1.0, with an equal likelihood of each value in that range occurring. A simulation using such a random number generator on the above discrete probability distribution is illustrated in Figure 8–2.

That procedure is repeated some large number of times—two hundred for example. The results are then summarized graphically or in the form of expected cash flow and standard deviation. Since the random number is equally likely to fall at any point between 0.0 and 1.0, there is a 0.25 probability that a cash inflow of $20,000 will be selected for a particular period, a 0.60 (0.85–0.25) probability that a cash inflow of $50,000 will be selected, and a 0.15 probability that a $100,000 inflow will be selected. Over a large number of repetitions, the proportion of

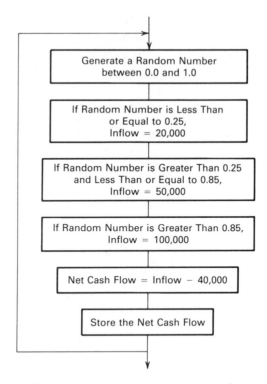

FIGURE 8-2 Flow Chart for Monte Carlo
Simulation

times a particular inflow is selected will approximately equal the probability of that inflow occurring.

It would have been much simpler to compute the possible net cash flows and their probabilities directly. But the benefits of the approach used will become obvious as additional random variables are considered.

Suppose we now decide to deal with uncertainty concerning cash outflows as well. Cash outflow could be any value between $20,000 and $60,000. The distribution is continuous, but probability estimates have been made for various ranges. These are as follows.

Cash Outflow Range	Probability
20,000 < Cash outflow < 30,000	0.2
30,000 < Cash outflow < 40,000	0.4
40,000 < Cash outflow < 50,000	0.3
50,000 < Cash outflow < 60,000	0.1

To use the Monte Carlo simulation approach, probabilities of points rather than ranges are needed. These are found by simply attributing the probability of each range to the midpoint for that range. Thus, the discrete approximation to the above continuous distribution is

Cash Outflow	Probability
25,000	0.2
35,000	0.4
45,000	0.3
55,000	0.1

This conversion to a discrete approximation makes it possible to use a random number generator exactly as was done before for discrete cash inflow possibilities.

Suppose now that you wish to forecast the probability distribution of cumulative net cash flows by month for the next three months. The steps involved are as follows:

1. Use a random number generator to select a cash inflow for the first month.
2. Use a random number generator to select a cash outflow for the first month.
3. Subtract cash outflow from cash inflow to compute net cash flow.
4. Record and store the cash flow for the first month.
5. Repeat steps 1 through 4 for the second month.
6. Repeat steps 1 through 4 for the third month.
7. Add cash flow for first and second months to get the cumulative cash flow for the first two months.
8. Add cash flow for the first, second, and third months to get the cumulative cash flow for the three months.
9. Record the cumulative cash flows.
10. Repeat steps 1 through 9 several hundred times, recording cash flow by month and cumulative cash flow for two and three months each time.
11. Summarize the results either graphically or in terms of mean and standard deviation.

A BASIC language computer program for the problem appears in Table 8-2, and the results appear in Table 8-3.

When first exposed to Monte Carlo simulation, people are frequently concerned about the loss of accuracy when going from a continuous distribution to a discrete approximation. In fact, the loss of accuracy is not a serious problem. Any desired accuracy level can be achieved by simply increasing the number of discrete approximations.

Table 8-2
BASIC PROGRAM FOR MONTE CARLO SIMULATION OF CASH FLOWS

```
10  RANDOM
20  DIM A(9)
30  FOR I = 1 TO 500
40  FOR J = 1 TO 3
60  LET X = RND(0)
70  IF X=<.25 THEN LET A(J) = 20000
80  IF .25<X AND X=<.85 THEN LET A(J) = 50000
90  IF X>.85 THEN LET A(J) = 100000
100 LET X = RND(0)
110 IF X=<.2 THEN LET A(J) = A(J)-25000
120 IF X>.2 AND X=<.6 THEN LET A(J) = A(J)-35000
130 IF X>.6 AND X=<.9 THEN LET A(J) = A(J)-45000
140 IF X>.9 THEN LET A(J) = A(J)-55000
150 NEXT J
160 LET A(3) = A(1) + A(2) + a(3)
170 LET A(2) = A(1) + A(2)
180 FOR J = 4 TO 6
190 LET A(J) = A(J) + A(J-3)
200 LET A(J+3) = A(J+3) + A(J-3)*A(J-3)
210 NEXT J
220 PRINT "ITERATION # ";I
230 NEXT I
240 FOR J = 4 TO 6
250 LET A(J+3) = SQR(A(J+3)/500 - (A(J)/500)*(A(J)/500))
260 NEXT J
270 PRINT "MONTH(S)  EXPECTED CUMULATIVE  STANDARD
DEVIATION"
280 PRINT "          CASH FLOW
290 PRINT "ONE     ", A(4)/500,A(7)
300 PRINT "TWO     ", A(5)/500,A(8)
310 PRINT "THREE   ", A(6)/500,A(9)
320 END
```

Table 8-3
MONTE CARLO SIMULATION OF CASH FLOWS

Month(s)	Expected Cumulative Cash Flow	Standard Deviation
One	11140	26017.3
Two	24550	37271.9
Three	36300	45744.0

As an example of how accuracy can be maintained, assume that cash sales for a particular company are normally distributed[1] with a mean of $100,000 and a standard deviation of $10,000. The normal distribution is symmetrical, meaning, for example, that the probability of sales exceeding the expected value by $10,000 is exactly the same as the probability of their falling $10,000 below the expected value. According to the table of the normal distribution (Appendix D), there is a 0.34 probability of sales falling between the mean and one standard deviation above the mean, a 0.48 probability of sales falling between the mean and two standard deviations above. Thus, there is a 0.14 (0.48 − 0.34) probability of sales being more than one standard deviation above the mean and less than two standard deviations above. The probability of sales being between the mean and three standard deviations above approaches 0.50. Thus, the probability of sales between two and three standard deviations above the mean is 0.02 (0.50 − 0.48). Since probabilities below the mean are the mirror of those above, the discrete approximation to this distribution would be

Sales Level	Probability
75,000	0.02
85,000	0.14
95,000	0.34
105,000	0.34
115,000	0.14
125,000	0.02

If this discrete approximation does not seem accurate enough, the number of intervals can simply be increased from six to some greater number, say twenty. This would give ten ranges on each side of the mean and would reduce each range from one standard deviation to 0.3 standard deviations. The discrete approximation computations would then be as follows

1. Range from mean less 3.0 standard deviations to mean less 2.7 standard deviations:
   A. Probability of sales between mean and mean less three standard deviations: *0.500*
   B. Probability of sales between mean and mean less 2.7 standard deviations: *0.497*
   C. Probability of sales between 2.7 and 3.0 standard deviations below the mean: 0.500 − 0.497 = 0.003

[1] See page 174 for a description of the normal distribution.

D. Midpoint of the range = mean − 2.85 standard deviations
$$= 100{,}000 - 2.85 \times 10{,}000$$
$$= 71{,}500$$

2. Range from mean less 2.7 standard deviations to mean less 2.4 standard deviations.
(Repeat calculation procedure as before.)

The above procedure would be repeated for each of the twenty ranges, and the more detailed discrete approximation would be

Sales	Probability
71,500	0.003
73,000	0.005
74,500	0.010
etc.	

Thus, the discrete approximation can be made as close an approximation as desired, by simply increasing the number of ranges that are being approximated.

The Use of Simulation Models

Two major issues in the development and use of simulation models are appropriate level of detail and verification. These issues are discussed in the following paragraphs.

At the point of moving from general to specific relationships, models frequently become so overwhelming that the project is abandoned. The deterministic model used for illustration contains one equation for variable costs and one for fixed costs. Certainly, there are dozens if not hundreds of costs in each category. A separate statement for each cost could easily increase the size of the model from six to six hundred statements, and virtually assure that the modeling project would be abandoned long before it was completed.

Excessively complex models have disadvantages beyond the cost of development They tend to provide such a mass of output that the user is swamped by results and finds it impossible to focus on the important parts. One oil company built a wonderfully complete financial model that provided hundreds of pages of computer printout about the company's projected financial characteristics. Despite tremendous development costs, the model was soon abandoned because the mass of information overwhelmed potential users. Every statement adds a cost in terms of time used. For the statement to be included, it must provide a return by increasing accuracy or by providing information that is important to the user. The model can be kept to a manageable size by reducing the set of statements to only those that are clearly needed.

Experience with models of both companies and the economy has shown that the benefits of increased detail decline rapidly as size increases. Models of twenty to thirty equations have frequently been found to be as accurate as models ten times as large.

Before a model is put into use, it should be verified. One method of verification is to run the model with data from some past period and compare results of the model to the actual outcome. Unfortunately, this cannot be done in many cases. A model may be of a new structure, making a historical test impossible. Probability models can seldom be tested against past results because the probability model works with a probability distribution and only one point on that distribution actually occurred last period. When verification through use of historical data is not possible, the model can still be verified in reference to its logic. The model must be studied carefully to determine if it actually is a proper description of the system under study. Careful documentation of the model is necessary to carry out this step and to keep the model useful with the passage of time.

This chapter is designed to serve as an introduction to the potentials for and principles of modeling and simulation. One who ends up using these techniques frequently will soon find that additional references are needed. The manuals that come with the electronic worksheet programs are the first additional reading source needed. Beyond these, a book on modeling will eventually prove useful. A good book for this purpose is

Wheelwright, Steven C. and Spyros G. Makridakis. *Computer Aided Modeling for Managers.* Reading, Mass.: Addison-Wesley, 1972.

9

DATA FOR FORECASTING

The most time-consuming part of the forecasting project is frequently the collection and preparation of information. Some data, such as information about populations and national or local economic conditions must be located in published sources. Data related to a specific company or organization is generally assembled by the forecaster. Whether data is collected from public sources or assembled by the forecaster, various adjustments may be required before it can be used. This chapter covers public sources of data and the preparation of data for use in forecasting.

PUBLICLY AVAILABLE DATA

When it is available, data from published sources is generally preferred over that collected by the forecaster. Publicly available data can be assembled quickly and is generally cheaper to use. Furthermore, much (but not all) publicly available data has been painstakingly verified to assure accuracy.

A listing of the data available to the forecaster would require several volumes. The libraries are filled with billions of bits of historical data covering at least some aspect of nearly every imaginable topic. Furthermore, forecasts are available on a variety of topics of general interest. For those items not found in the libraries, private associations and computerized services allow the forecaster to tap additional data banks. In this section, the primary sources are outlined and ways are suggested for the forecaster to become familiar with his area of interest. As a further aid, Appendix B is an annotated bibliography of some major data sources which are arranged according to frequency of use.

Primary Sources of Publicly Available Data

The U.S. government is by far the largest collector and publisher of data in the country. Regardless of the problem being addressed, the U.S. government probably collects and publishes at least some related data. A brief listing of the major U.S. government data sources is included in Appendix B. From these sources the forecaster will find references to additional information in his particular area of interest. Every large city in the United States has at least one library designated as a U.S. government depository. These libraries have the more extensive collections of data assembled by the U.S. government.

The two sources most widely used by business forecasters are the *Statistical Abstract of the United States,* published annually, and the *Survey of Current Business,* published monthly. The *Abstract* is a general source of statistics on all topics and serves as a guide to which agencies furnish which data. The *Survey* presents detailed data on economic activity.

In addition to Appendix B and the *Abstract,* there are two other resources that can be used in finding the right source for data compiled by the U.S. government. The first of these is a librarian. Many good libraries have a government documents librarian who specializes in compiling materials published by the U.S. government. As the government document filing system is somewhat complex, the services of the government documents librarian are quite beneficial.

The *American Statistics Index* is another source that is extremely helpful in locating statistics published by the U.S. government. For example, a forecaster interested in corn production could find listed in the *Index* eight U.S. government publications in which corn production and corn price statistics appear. Time spent developing an understanding of U.S. government sources will be rewarded in terms of quick access to a vast amount of relevant data.

State and local government units also compile and make available a large amount of data. While most U.S. government data of interest are published and on file in libraries, a significant amount of data compiled by state and local governments is not in published form. These data, collected for specific purposes and available to people wishing to use them for other purposes, are not published because demand is insufficient. Because many of the data are not published, some telephone calling and digging is frequently required. Most states and many municipalities have industrial development agencies that work to attract new business to the area. These agencies are very helpful in providing data they have available and in finding data that may be housed in other places in the governmental unit. Regulatory agencies and taxing authorities also have data bases that are frequently of interest to the forecaster. Things such as the amount of energy used or the volume of consumer lending are available from regulatory agencies. Local sales and income data are available from local taxing authorities.

Other Suppliers of State and Local Data

In addition to local governmental units, a number of other organizations provide data on local and regional bases. Chambers of Commerce, interested in providing services to their members and in attracting new business to the area, have assembled extensive data about the local community. Some commercial banks also maintain economic research units and willingly supply local data. Each of the above mentioned sources will already have the advantage of being familiar with local data sources and can probably point out sources of data if they cannot furnish the data themselves.

Much of the data published by the federal government is also broken down by state or city. *Statistics of Income,* a publication of the Internal Revenue Service, contains data on income breakdown by localities. The Bureau of the Census also publishes data on areas as small as a few square blocks. The *County and City Data Book* is a helpful source of data on a regional basis.

Private associations are another useful source of data on both a national and a local basis. As mentioned earlier, Chambers of Commerce and commercial banks frequently supplement the efforts of local governments in providing data on business-related factors. Special interest associations such as the Tax Foundation also collect and publish data of interest to members. Finally, many industry associations collect data related to their industry. Some of this information is available in widely published sources such as the *Savings and Loan Fact Book* and the *Life Insurance Fact Book.* Other information is available only to members of the association. Even the associations that publish data for the general public will attempt to answer special requests from members. Because they are supported by contributions, these associations are eager to show that they are of service to members. The *Encyclopedia of Associations* provides the names and addresses of 13,589 national associations, ranging from major groups such as the federated American Trucking Associations to highly specialized organizations such as the Guitar and Accessories Manufacturers of America and the National Association of Left-Handed Golfers.

Commercial services also provide the forecaster with a large amount of useful information. For example, Moody's, Standard and Poor's, and Value Line are services that provide large amounts of information concerning the financial markets, individual companies, and individual securities. The Survey Research Center at the University of Michigan makes public the results of a number of surveys of consumer attitudes and plans. Predicasts is a service that specializes in compiling forecasts from other sources and making them available in one publication. Leading commercial services are outlined in Appendix B.

Computerized services also provide important information. We are just entering the phase of rapid growth in computer data systems. These systems consist of large computers that contain massive amounts of information which can be accessed by computer terminals or personal computers with the ability to communicate with other computers over telephone lines. In some cases the data banks can even be accessed by a television without benefit of a personal computer or a computer terminal. While the data contained in the various data banks vary widely, stock market and economic data are the most widely available. With most of these data banks, the potential user pays an initial fee of $100 to $200 to be allowed to use the service and then an hourly fee varying from $5 to $300 per hour for the time the service is actually used. Some libraries have access to one or more of these services. The library terminal can be used if access is infrequent.

While the hourly costs of these might initially seem to be high, a large amount of data can be acquired in a short time. Thus, total costs are usually reasonable. When one considers that the primary cost of many forecasting projects is the cost of time used to assemble data, these computerized data banks frequently turn out to be very cost effective. Several of the major computerized sources are listed in Appendix B. Complete listings can be found in the *Encyclopedia of Information Systems* (see Appendix B).

Accuracy and Meaning of Published Data

While accuracy problems are generally no greater—and frequently less severe—for published data than for data developed by the forecaster, it is a mistake to assume that data is accurate just because it has been published. Mistakes can be made and data collection methods are sometimes faulty—frequently on purpose to support a particular point of view.

There are several methods of verifying published data. One approach is to contact those responsible for the data and find out how it was collected and compiled. A second approach is to compare data from two different sources. Suppose one wishes to study past movements of long-term interest rates. The Moody's Investor Service series can be compared with the Standard and Poor's Investor Service series to see if there are any significant differences. A third approach is to check for outliers—numbers outside the expected range. For the interest rates previously discussed, one might find the largest period-to-period changes and make sure these are not errors. Another approach is to randomly select data points and reconstruct the data to see if you get the same figures. In the final analysis, even after all possible checking has been done, the forecaster will still keep in mind the possibility that the data are wrong.

In addition to the problem of recording errors, there is the question of whether the data actually means what you think it does. For example, unemployment figures are meaningless if one does not know how an unemployed person is defined. Published sources such as *Readings in Concepts and Methods of National Income Statistics* frequently provide the necessary background information. Other times it is necessary to contact the person compiling the data. The *Federal Statistical Directory* lists personnel responsible for compilation of various statistics published by the U.S. government and can be used to find out whom to contact for clarification. The existence of this volume attests to extent of needs for clarification.

A few hours at the local library examining some of the sources listed in Appendix B will be rewarded with access to a massive data set. If the cautions discussed above are observed, this data will be extremely useful for forecasting.

PRIVATE DATA

In addition to data collected from public sources, the forecaster will need data about the specific situation—the company's costs, customers, etc. Proper selection and management of the needed data base has a major impact on the cost and accuracy of forecasts.

Like knowledge of publicly available sources, knowledge of the private data base will evolve with the forecaster's experience and recognition of needs. While the particular data in the private data base will vary according to specific needs, there are guidelines that should be followed in the establishment of any data base:

1. Collect only needed data. It takes time to assemble data and time is a scarce resource. A plan of operation for the forecast should be a guide to what data is collected. Following this guideline avoids the expense and confusion of excess data and assures that the necessary data will be available.

2. Maximum use should be made of data that is publicly available. While this may sound obvious, it is not unusual to find raw data being assembled when the desired data is already available from some public source. The data can be obtained much more quickly and economically if public sources are used.

3. Data should be stored in the most disaggregated form possible. Much data already in existence come in the form of accounting entries which are originally recorded as single transactions. Other data sources, such as surveys, begin with data collected in the form of individual responses. Since data is originally collected in the form of single observations, it should be maintained in this form. Data may be first aggregated for one purpose, such as preparation of an annual income statement. Another person may later be interested in other factors, such as the relationship between advertising campaigns in an area and orders placed. This person would need to look at the orders—the original document—and aggregate them by date and advertising market. This cannot be done with the data aggregated for some other purpose.

4. Data must be documented carefully. Most forecasters and statistical researchers have learned this lesson the hard way. A set of data is left on the desk with the forecaster relying on memory for the exact meaning of the numbers. Returning to the project a few days or a week later, the forecaster receives a painful lesson in the limits of human memory. If data are not carefully documented, they may as well be discarded.

5. Data must be verified before being used. Data should be assumed to be inaccurate until accuracy is assured.

6. Data systems should be designed to allow for expansion. A good rule of system design in general, and forecasting data system design in particular, is to allow for the addition of more data to the base. This is a good idea even if the data are originally gathered for a one-time forecast. If one is using three variables to forecast sales, he may later decide to use five. And the most current data will be added to the file as they become available. The data storage method should be designed to allow for these additions.

CONVERTING DATA TO USABLE FORM

Many times data is not found in the form that is most useful to the forecaster. In some cases, a relatively simple conversion will greatly increase its usefulness. These conversions are covered in the following paragraphs.

Summary Statistics

Suppose one has available as data the number of hours of television watched per week for 2,000 people for each of 200 weeks. These 400,000 observations must be condensed and summarized to be meaningful.

The mean and standard deviation—introduced and explained in Appendix A—are the two most widely used summary statistics. These two numbers give a good picture of the characteristics of the population. Two-thirds of a normally distributed population[1] lies within ± one standard deviation of the mean, 95 percent lie within ± two standard deviations, and 99.7 percent lie within ± three standard deviations. If a particular population exhibits normally distributed television viewing patterns with a mean of 13.3 hours per week and a standard deviation of three hours, two-thirds of the population watches between 11.3 and 16.3 hours, 95 percent of the population watches between 7.3 and 19.3 hours, and 99.7 percent of the population watches between 4.3 and 22.3 hours.

Unfortunately, data are not always normally distributed. Miles driven each year by a particular group provides such an example:

Miles Driven per Year		
At Least	But Less Than	Percentage of Group
25,000 and more		10
20,000	25,000	10
15,000	20,000	25
10,000	15,000	20
5,000	10,000	20
1,000	5,000	10
0	1,000	5

[1]See page 174 for a description of the normal distribution.

It is not possible to compute mean miles driven from this data because nothing is known about average miles driven by those who drive 25,000 or more miles per year. In addition, the distribution of miles driven does not appear to be normal. In this case, the median is a more useful measure. The median is the level such that half of the values are greater and half are less. In this case, the median would be between 10,000 and 15,000. The formula for estimating the median for data reported in groups, as was done in this case, is

$$\text{Median} = L + \frac{0.50 - P_b}{P_m}(U - L) \tag{9-1}$$

where

L = lower limit of the range in which the median falls;

U = upper limit of the range in which the median falls;

P_b = percentage of the total below the range in which the median falls; and

P_m = percentage of the total in the range in which the median falls.

For example, the estimated median mileage is

$$\text{Median} = 10,000 + \frac{0.50 - 0.35}{0.20}(15,000 - 10,000) = 13,750$$

As an alternative to the standard deviation, the upper and lower quartiles may be used as measures of spread. The upper quartile is the value that 25 percent of the observations are above: it is the median of the upper half. Likewise, the lower quartile is the value that 25 percent of the observations are below. The upper and lower quartiles of classified data such as the automobile mileage numbers are found by finding the medians of the upper and lower halves. For example, the upper quartile is

$$\text{Upper quartile} = 15,000 + \frac{0.75 - 0.55}{0.25}(20,000 - 15,000) = 19,000 \text{ miles}$$

The use of summary statistics makes it possible to reduce thousands of observations to a few numbers. The forecaster frequently wishes to forecast averages or medians. Furthermore, these summary statistics are frequently used even when individual items are to be forecast. For example, sales for a single company may be forecast based on average use of the product per person or median disposable income.

Conversion to Growth-Related Numbers

It is sometimes more meaningful to forecast the growth rate of some series than the series itself. Likewise, the growth rate of some explanatory variable may be more important that the absolute level of the variable. Growth can be stated in either unit or percentage terms. Table 9-1 shows a series of observations with the data converted to unit growth and to percentage growth.

Growth rates are useful in many forecasting situations. First, if the growth rate is constant, one can forecast by assuming that the growth rate will continue. Second, the growth rate of some factors has more impact than the absolute levels. Interest rate forecasters, for example, watch the growth in the money supply more closely than they watch the absolute level.

To compute the average unit growth per period for longer periods, it is only necessary to compute the mean of the unit growth numbers or use the formula:

$$\overline{d} = (E - B)/k \qquad (9\text{-}2)$$

where

d = average unit growth;

E = ending value;

B = beginning value; and

k = the number of periods between the beginning and ending observation.

Table 9-1
GROWTH RATE ANALYSIS

Raw Data	Unit Growth	Percentage Growth
17,298		
18,378	1,080	0.062
19,504	1,126	0.061
20,724	1,220	0.063
22,014	1,290	0.062
23,358	1,344	0.061
24,827	1,469	0.063
26,385	1,558	0.063
27,995	1,610	0.061

For the example in Table 9-1, the average unit growth would be:

$$\overline{d} = (27{,}995 - 17{,}298)/8 = 1{,}337$$

Note, however, that unit growth is not stable in this example, but steadily increases from year to year.

The average percentage growth is frequently more useful, but care must be used in computation or misleading information will result. The problem involved is illustrated with the following example.

Period	1	2	3
Value	100	150	90
Percentage growth		0.50	−0.40

The average of +50 percent and −40 percent is 5 percent. However, the value actually decreased from 100 to 90. Thus, the average percentage growth of 0.05 does not reflect realized growth. The following formula gives a more accurate picture of the realized average percentage growth (R). The terms mean the same things they did in equation 9-2.

$$R = {}^{k}\!\sqrt{E/B} - 1.0 \qquad\qquad (9\text{-}3)$$

For the three observations above, the realized average percentage return is

$$R = {}^{2}\!\sqrt{90/100} - 1 = -5.1\%$$

This gives a clearer picture of realized growth than a simple mathematical average of percentage growth rates.

The average realized growth rate for the data in Table 9-1 is

$$R = {}^{8}\!\sqrt{27{,}995/17{,}298} - 1.0 = 6.203\%$$

Stock prices provide a good example of actual use of growth figures in testing forecasting techniques. The security analyst needs to forecast at least the direction, and preferably the amount, of change in stock prices. The Dow Jones Industrial Average, a widely quoted stock price index, rose from 167 in 1926 to 1060 in 1982. Gross National Product has risen similarly over that time, as has population, wheat production, and dog ownership. Because time has passed and all of these variables have generally increased, the relationships are clouded; one may conclude that some unrelated factor such as dog ownership causes stock prices to change. While stock prices have shown a tendency to increase over time—an average period-to-period growth greater than zero—examination of the percentage growth numbers reveals a random pattern around the average growth rate. Factors such as Gross National Product change are useless in projecting changes in stock prices because stock prices change in anticipation of things that affect the stockholders' earnings.

Smoothing Data

Many times, the underlying pattern is clouded by the impacts of one-time random shocks, missing data, and erroneously recorded information. A forecaster working with sales of an office equipment manufacturer in Chicago may find the data clouded by strikes, snow storms, and large but infrequent government orders. In order to determine the relationship between sales and factors such as business conditions, it will be helpful to develop some method of filtering out the noise so that the underlying pattern can be seen. Several methods are suggested in the following paragraphs.

Freehand smoothing is one approach to eliminating noise. If first-quarter sales were distorted by a large one-time order, the impact of the one-time order can simply be subtracted from total sales. If a strike occurred in the fourth quarter, average fourth-quarter sales for previous years, plus a factor to adjust for any growth trend, can be substituted for actual fourth-quarter sales. This type of adjustment is referred to as freehand smoothing because it is common practice to begin with a graphical presentation of the data and then use visual inspection to identify and adjust for nonrecurring events. Figure 9-1 contains a time series of sales and also shows the same series smoothed to eliminate the impacts of nonrecurring events.

Moving averages are another approach to damping the effects of random events. To use a moving average, one replaces the value of the series for each period with the average value of the series for some number of periods ending in that period. Below is an example of a series converted to a four-period moving average.

Series	90	115	121	103	108	137	143	121	126	159
Four-period moving average				107	112	117	123	127	132	137

The moving average for the last period, for example, is computed as $(143 + 121 + 126 + 159)/4 = 137$. The series represents quarterly data. Converting it to a four-quarter moving average removes the impact of

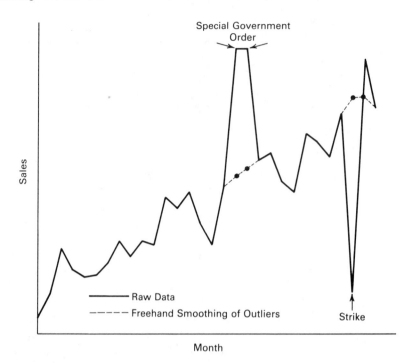

FIGURE 9-1 Freehand Smoothing

seasonal factors and makes it possible to see the long-term trend in the data quite clearly.

Moving averages are used to filter out cyclical factors and to dampen the impact of random events Figure 9-2 shows the data from Figure 9-1 smoothed with moving averages of various lengths. A moving average is quite effective in damping the effects of small random events, but will not eliminate the effects of large nonrecurring events. Frequently, the large shocks are dealt with and then a moving average is computed.

Index Construction

A large volume of data is sometimes made meaningful by conversion to a single index. The impact of inflation is summarized in the form of a consumer price index, and stock prices are summarized in the form of an index such as the Dow Jones Industrial Average. Many forecasters also construct their own indices for particular purposes. For example, an index of residential construction for a particular area may be maintained by a forecaster interested in predicting demand for roofing material of a type primarily used in residential construction.

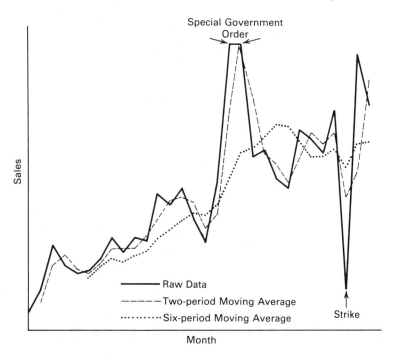

FIGURE 9-2 Moving Average Smoothing

There are two general types of indices, and a particular index may be a combination of the two. A ratio index simply expresses a number as a ratio of some other series or the same series at an earlier time. A composite index combines many diverse observations into a single number. The consumer price index is a combination of the two, being an average of prices stated as a ratio to average prices at an earlier time.

Ratio Index

As an example of a ratio index, consider productivity experience with new factories. For various reasons, productivity per man hour is generally lower during early months of operation, only reaching normal levels after bugs have been worked out and workers have learned their jobs. As part of the process of evaluating new plant proposals, Consolidated Manufacturing Corporation wants to forecast the pattern of productivity growth for new plants. This is a bit difficult since each plant produces related but somewhat different products. Table 9-2 contains unit output and labor input for the last four plants opened by the company.

Table 9-2
PRODUCTIVITY EXPERIENCE OF CONSOLIDATED MANUFACTURING COMPANY

Month	Plant A Unit Output	Plant A Man Hours	Plant B Unit Output	Plant B Man Hours	Plant C Unit Output	Plant C Man Hours	Plant D Unit Output	Plant D Man Hours
1	284	200,000	1,000	250,000	577	200,000	156	100,000
2	760	300,000	2,520	350,000	1,123	220,000	565	200,000
3	1,195	350,000	4,148	425,000	1,703	250,000	1,157	300,000
4	1,643	400,000	5,900	500,000	2,234	275,000	1,877	400,000
5	2,091	450,000	7,392	550,000	2,740	300,000	2,955	550,000
6	2,540	500,000	8,856	600,000	3,221	325,000	4,149	700,000
7	2,842	525,000	10,112	640,000	3,678	350,000	5,101	800,000
8	3,124	550,000	11,315	680,000	4,058	370,000	5,731	850,000
9	3,389	575,000	12,470	720,000	4,415	390,000	6,336	900,000
10	3,632	600,000	13,395	750,000	4,637	400,000	6,845	940,000
11	3,712	600,000	14,167	775,000	4,721	400,000	7,292	975,000
12	3,772	600,000	14,896	800,000	4,785	400,000	7,638	1,000,000
Engineering Standard	4,000	600,000	16,000	800,000	5,000	400,000	8,333	1,000,000

The data would be more useful if they were converted to some sort of utilization index. A convenient labor utilization index can be constructed by dividing the actual hours per unit for each period at each plant by the engineering standard for that plant. Thus, the formula is

$$L_t = H_t/H_s \qquad (9\text{-}4)$$

where

L_t = the labor utilization index for a particular plant t periods after start-up;

H_t = man hours per unit produced in the plant in period t; and

H_s = the engineering standard for the plant.

For plant A in month 1, man hours per unit produced are 704 (200,000/284), and the labor utilization index is

$$L_1 = 704/150 = 4.69$$

In other words, man hours per unit in the first period are 4.69 times the engineering standard. For plant C in month 10, the labor utilization index is

$$L_{10} = 86.26/80 = 1.08$$

or 1.08 times the engineering standard. Figure 9-3 shows the labor utilization indices for each of the four plants for the second through twelfth months of operation.

The construction of a proper index goes a long way toward solving this particular forecasting problem. First, the labor utilization indices for all plants follow similar patterns (see Figure 9-3). Second, the labor utilization index is higher for large plants, with plant size measured in man hours per month. Thus, one can forecast the labor utilization index for each month of the first year by looking at Figure 9-3 and selecting the pattern for a plant similar in size to the one being considered. For example, if a 900,000 man hour plant were being considered, the labor utilization index for each month would be halfway between those for plants B and D.

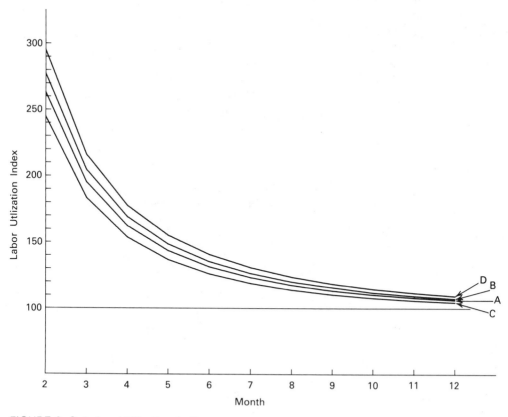

FIGURE 9-3 Labor Utilization Indices

As is true of all indices, there was nothing magic about the particular type of index chosen in this example. The purpose of this index, or any other index, is to convert observations to the form that will be most useful.

Composite Indices

Composite indices are used to combine a number of observations into a single number. Generally, a composite index is used to compare a combination of values for one period with the same combination for previous periods. The consumer price index, for example, is a composite index of prices of various goods and services; it is the ratio of the cost of a market basket of goods and services to its price at a specified base time.

To illustrate the construction of a composite index, consider a boat manufacturing company that uses three major inputs: labor, aluminum, and electricity. The company's most popular boat requires twenty hours of labor, two units of aluminum, and two units of electricity. The ratios of inputs are about the same for all boats manufactured by the company. The prices for the various inputs, and the computations of price indices, appear in Table 9-3.

The 1978 cost was 112 percent of the 1977 cost and the 1979 cost was 122 percent of the 1977 cost (see Table 9-3). Forecasting this index would be one way to forecast manufacturing costs.

While the mathematics of index construction are relatively straightforward, there are some difficult interpretation problems.

Table 9-3
BOAT MANUFACTURING COST INDEX

	Units Used	1977		1978		1979	
		Unit Cost	Total Cost	Unit Cost	Total Cost	Unit Cost	Total Cost
Labor	20	$ 10	$200	$ 11	$220	$ 12	$240
Aluminum	2	100	200	110	220	115	230
Electricity	2	50	100	60	120	70	140
Total cost per boat			$500		$560		$610

Index:
  1977: 500/500 = 1.00
  1978: 560/500 = 1.12
  1979: 610/500 = 1.22

These can be illustrated with a discussion of the consumer price index. As was done for the cost index in Table 9-3, the price index represents the price of a certain package of goods at different times. A problem is that the package of goods people buy changes from place to place. The price of wool suits may be higher in Hawaii than in Chicago, but Hawaiians do not buy wool suits. Does a cost comparison based on a common market basket provide a reasonable comparison between Chicago and Honolulu? If a different market basket is used for each market, are the numbers comparable? Tastes and needs differ over time as well as between locations. A price index including buggies and washboards while excluding automobiles and washing machines would hardly be meaningful. On the other hand, it is difficult to compare costs between times when different market baskets are used. At best, it is difficult to create a composite index that provides a stable picture over extended periods of time and over different situations. The users of published indices must be constantly aware of the methods of construction and limitations on comparability.

SUMMARY

Every forecaster must locate, verify, and modify data to meet particular needs. Many forecasters must also develop and manage a private data base. The guidelines in this chapter are useful in developing and maintaining forecasting data.

PROBLEMS

1. Find the estimates of the consumer price inflation rate for the past year as constructed by the Bureau of Labor Statistics (the familiar consumer price index) and as constructed by the Department of Commerce for use in adjusting GNP accounts for inflation. Find out how the two estimates are computed. Which measure gives the most accurate representation of the change in the cost of living for the average American.

2. Shown below is information on the number of meals eaten outside the home each month for people in a particular area. Compute the median, upper quartile, and lower quartile.

Number of meals	0–10	11–20	21–30	31–40	over 40
Percentage of people	30	20	15	10	25

3. Express the growth pattern of the following data in what you think is the most usable form.

Period	1	2	3	4	5	6	7	8	9	10
Value	1,000	1,100	1,210	1,331	1,464	1,527	1,670	1,837	2,140	2,359

4. Following is a set of data on monthly shipments from a factory. The factory suffered a strike in the seventh period. Smooth the data in a way you feel would be most appropriate and prepare a projection for period 21.

Period	Shipments	Period	Shipments
1	1,000	11	1,201
2	1,017	12	1,221
3	1,043	13	1,239
4	1,060	14	1,259
5	1,078	15	1,280
6	1,110	16	1,298
7	1,080	17	1,298
8	1,160	18	1,323
9	1,162	19	1,341
10	1,178	20	1,381

5. Shown below are data on costs and usage of the only three products purchased by a particular group of consumers. Construct a consumer price index of the form you feel would most reasonably reflect consumer costs.

Year	Cost per Unit			Units Purchased per Consumer		
	X	Y	Z	X	Y	Z
1975	$12	$36	$18	100	100	100
1976	12.5	38	19	105	105	105
1977	13.2	40	25	110	107	90
1978	14.0	41.5	32	130	110	60
1979	14.8	44	46	150	118	40
1980	15.5	46	72	180	125	10

10

EVALUATING FORECAST ACCURACY

Every forecast should be supplemented with an assessment of the accuracy that can be expected. This is essential if planning is to allow for a reasonable margin for error. If forecasts are being made on a repetitive basis, their accuracy should be continually monitored to make sure the forecasting method is working and to spot opportunities for improving accuracy.

Many forecasting projects are repetitive, with a new forecast being prepared on a regular basis, such as weekly or monthly. Past forecasts and actual outcomes provide a basis for evaluating forecast accuracy. If a forecast is being prepared only once or is being prepared for the first time, a holdout approach can often be used to achieve the same result. Suppose, for example, that one hundred periods of historical data are available. The first sixty might be used to develop the model, with the most recent forty periods being used to compare the model's forecasts to actual outcomes. When a series of forecasts can be compared to actual observations, a number of methods can be used to evaluate forecast accuracy. Even in the absence of a set of past forecasts and actual outcomes, there are still some things that can be said about forecast accuracy. Explicit analysis of accuracy will increase the usefulness of present forecasts and improve the accuracy of future forecasts.

In this chapter, the three primary approaches to forecast accuracy evaluation are covered. The graphical methods of displaying past forecasting results are used to help the forecaster pinpoint problems and potential ways of increasing accuracy. Statistical methods provide numerical measures of accuracy that are particularly helpful in comparing forecasting methods and in establishing confidence ranges for new forecasts. Subjective methods involve identifying the possible factors that could lead to the outcome's being different from the forecast. Each of these approaches should be thought of as complementary; they can be used in combination to provide a solid approach to the evaluation of forecast accuracy.

GRAPHICAL METHODS

Even though a forecaster may be skilled in the use of statistical methods, a graphical display of forecasting errors can be a powerful aid in identifying potential problems and in revising forecasting methods. The graphical methods are particularly helpful in identifying problems as early as possible and in deciding what types of problems need to be addressed in revision of the forecasting method. They are also quite useful to the consumer of forecasts who wishes to systematically evaluate the quality of forecasts received.

Control Charts

The most widely used graphical approach is the control chart. It was developed to identify machines that needed adjustment and can be used to identify forecasting methods that need adjustment.

Table 10-1 contains actual and forecasted interest rates. Column 4 contains the errors and column 5 contains the cumulative errors. The cumulative errors from column 5 are presented in the form of a control chart in Figure 10-1. If there is no bias in the forecasting model, the cumulative errors should be close to zero. A pattern of cumulative errors moving regularly away from zero in either direction is a sign of bias; the forecasting method regularly overestimates or regularly underestimates the actual value. It is obvious from Figure 10-1 that some type of bias began to develop after 1973 and that the forecasting method should be revised.

One question faced when using the control chart is that of exactly when the cumulative errors have reached a level indicating the need for adjustment. As a practical matter, forecasters generally use two or three times the standard error as the control limit. The standard error for the forecasts in Table 10-1, based on periods before 1959, was 1.03. A control limit of twice the standard error was crossed in 1977. This

Table 10-1
INTEREST RATE FORECASTS

1 Year	2 Rate	3 Forecast	4 Difference	5 Cumulative Difference
1959	4.70	4.67	0.03	0.03
1960	4.76	4.47	0.29	0.32
1961	4.50	4.99	−0.49	−0.17
1962	4.34	5.06	−0.72	−0.89
1963	4.27	3.47	0.80	−0.09
1964	4.44	5.38	−0.94	−1.03
1965	4.54	4.32	0.22	−0.81
1966	5.42	4.52	0.90	0.09
1967	5.86	6.78	−0.92	−0.83
1968	6.48	6.83	−0.35	−1.18
1969	7.56	7.40	0.16	−1.02
1970	8.69	7.89	0.80	−0.22
1971	7.67	7.86	−0.19	−0.41
1972	7.42	7.30	0.12	−0.29
1973	7.74	7.65	0.09	−0.20
1974	9.04	7.72	1.32	1.12
1975	9.44	9.17	0.27	1.39
1976	8.92	8.43	0.49	1.88
1977	8.43	7.68	0.75	2.63
1978	8.97	7.19	1.78	4.41

crossing would signal a need to adjust the forecasting method. Following adjustment, the cumulative error would be reset to zero and the process started again.

Of course, the use of the control limit approach does not require that a chart be prepared. When a computerized forecasting approach is being used for a large number of items, such as inventory control, the computer can be programmed to maintain cumulative records of errors and to print a warning when a control limit is passed. Thus the forecaster managing hundreds of forecasts can quickly identify those in need of further refinement.

Prediction-Realization Diagram

The prediction-realization diagram is a graphical method of discovering the types of errors being made. Figure 10-2 is a prediction-realization diagram based on the data in Table 10-1. The horizontal axis

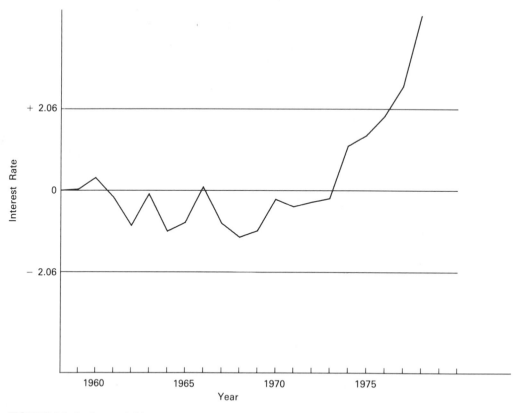

FIGURE 10-1 Control Chart

represents actual values and the vertical axis represents the forecasted value. An absolutely accurate forecast would fall on the 45° line. As is generally done when using the prediction-realization diagram, the actual values were restated in terms of changes from the previous period, and the forecasts were restated in terms of forecasted change from the previous period. Thus the diagram represents forecasted and actual change each period.

As shown in Figure 10-2, six types of errors are possible. Four types of errors represent overestimates and underestimates while two represent turning point errors—either prediction of a positive change when a negative change occurred or prediction of a negative change when a positive change occurred. Recognition of the types of errors being made is helpful in evaluating and refining the forecasting method. Frequent turning point errors, for example, would indicate a need to recognize either a cyclical component or additional explanatory variables.

The forecasted and actual values from Table 10-1 were converted to forecasted change and actual change, and then plotted in Figure 10-2. The circled dots represent the periods since 1973, when the control chart showed that the model was developing a systematic bias. The control chart shows that forecasts were continually below actual values in this period. The turning point errors were part of this bias; the model forecasted downturns that did not occur. Therefore, the bias is the error problem that needs to be dealt with. Either the relationship between interest rates and the explanatory variables has changed, or other explanatory variables must be added to the forecasting model.

QUANTITATIVE METHODS

Quantitative measures of forecast accuracy are useful in comparing forecasting methods and in making confidence interval estimates. Several quantitative methods are available, each of which is useful in

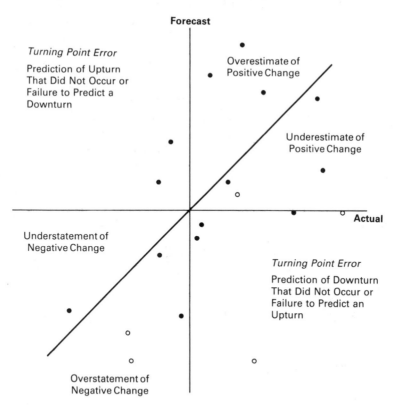

FIGURE 10-2 Prediction-Realization Diagram

159

certain situations. Methods of computation and guidelines for usage of each are covered in the following paragraphs.

Average Error

The average error, more correctly called the average absolute error or the mean absolute error, is the simplest measure to compute and explain to people not trained in statistics or forecasting methods. The formula for the average error is simply

$$\text{Average error} = [|F_1 - A_1| + |A_2 - A_2| + \ldots + |F_t - A_t|]/T \qquad (10\text{-}1)$$

where T is the number of forecasts to be used in the computation, F_t is the forecast for period t, and A_t is the actual value for period t. The pair of double vertical lines indicates the absolute value of the inclosed expression. The forecasted and actual values from Table 10-1 are reproduced in Table 10-2. The absolute values of the errors appear in column 4. The sum of these observations is divided by the number of observations to generate the average error of 0.58.

The average error can be compared with the average errors for other forecasting methods or with the average errors for other time periods. For example, the average error increased from 0.566 in the first ten years to 0.597 in the second ten years, indicating that the forecasts were not as accurate in the second ten years. While the average error can be presented alone as a representation of accuracy, it does not have statistical properties that make it useful in estimating confidence intervals for future forecasts. Other measures must be used for this purpose.

Standard Error

The standard error is the most widely used statistical measure of forecasting accuracy and has been used throughout this book. Its formula is

$$\text{Standard error} = \sqrt{[(F_1 - A_1)^2 + (F_2 - A_2)^2 + \ldots + (F_t - A_t)^2]/T} \qquad (10\text{-}2)$$

The standard error differs from the average error in two important ways. First, because the errors are squared during computation, the measure places relatively more emphasis on large errors. Second, the standard error can sometimes be used to compute confidence intervals for future forecasts.

Table 10-2
INTEREST RATE FORECASTS AND ERRORS

1 Year	2 Rate	3 Forecast	4 Difference	5 Difference Squared
1958	4.05			
1959	4.70	4.67	0.03	0.0009
1960	4.76	4.47	0.29	0.0841
1961	4.50	4.99	0.49	0.2401
1962	4.34	5.06	0.72	0.5184
1963	4.27	3.47	0.80	0.6400
1964	4.44	5.38	0.94	0.8836
1965	4.54	4.32	0.22	0.0484
1966	5.42	4.52	0.90	0.8100
1967	5.86	6.78	0.92	0.8464
1968	6.48	6.83	0.35	0.1225
1969	7.56	7.40	0.16	0.0256
1970	8.69	7.89	0.80	0.6400
1971	7.67	7.86	0.19	0.0361
1972	7.42	7.30	0.12	0.0144
1973	7.74	7.65	0.09	0.0081
1974	9.04	7.72	1.32	1.7424
1975	9.44	9.17	0.27	0.0729
1976	8.92	8.43	0.49	0.2401
1977	8.43	7.68	0.75	0.5625
1978	8.97	7.19	1.78	3.1684
Sum			11.63	10.7049
Sum/20			0.58	0.535
			Standard Error =	$\sqrt{0.535} = 0.732$

The standard error can be used for confidence interval estimation if: (1) the error terms are normally distributed;[1] (2) the average forecasting error is zero—that is, there is no tendency to regularly overestimate or underestimate; and (3) the errors are not serially correlated—that is, the error terms do not exhibit a pattern over time, with regard to either direction or size. If these conditions are met, it is expected that 68 percent of the outcomes will be within ± one standard error of the forecast, 95 percent will be within ± two times the standard error, and 99.7 percent will be within ± three times the standard error.

[1]See page 174 for a description of the normal distribution. Appendix D is a table of areas under the normal curve.

The error terms in Table 10-2 fail to meet the tests necessary for computation of confidence intervals. For example, it is clear from the control chart that there is a pattern in the error terms. However, they can be used as an illustration of the confidence limit computation. The standard error for the forecasts in Table 10-2 is 0.73. If the error terms satisfied the conditions listed above and the forecast for the next period was 8.32, there would be a 0.68 probability that the actual interest rate would be between 7.59 and 9.05 (8.32 ± 0.73), and a 0.95 probability that it would be between 6.86 and 9.78 (8.32 ± 2 × 0.73). Because the conditions for confidence interval estimation were not met in this case, the actual confidence intervals are probably larger, but the confidence range is not known.

Theil's *U*

Theil's *U* is an index of relative accuracy. It compares the accuracy of a forecasting model to forecasts from a naive model which merely uses this period's outcome as next period's forecast.

The formula for Theil's *U* is[2]

$$U = \frac{\text{Standard error of the forecasting model}}{\text{Standard error of the naive model}} \qquad (10\text{-}4)$$

A *U* greater than 1.0 indicates that the method was worse than the naive model, and a *U* of less than 1.0 indicates that it was better. A *U* of zero means that the forecasting model was perfect.

For the data in Table 10-2, the standard error was 0.732. The standard error of the naive model is

$$SE = \sqrt{[(4.70 - 4.05)^2 + (4.76 - 4.70)^2 + \ldots + (8.97 - 8.43)^2]/20}$$
$$= 0.641$$

The *U* is then 0.732/0.641 = 1.14

Clearly the forecasting model did not produce forecasts as accurate as those generated by the naive model.

The *U* can also be used to compare the accuracy of various forecasting methods or to compare the accuracy of one method in different time spans. For example, it is useful to compare accuracy by

[2]A more convenient computational formula is

$$U = \sqrt{[\sum_{t=2}^{n} (F_t - A_t)^2]/[\sum_{t=2}^{n} (A_t - A_{t-1})^2]}$$

dividing the data into two periods and computing two values for U. The U for 1959 through 1968 is 1.48, and the U for 1969 through 1978 is 0.99; the model produced better forecasts, relative to the naive model, in the latter period than in the former.

The U and the standard error frequently provide complementary information. The standard errors and Us for the first and second half of the period in Table 10-2 are

	U	Standard Error
1959–1968	1.48	0.648
1969–1978	0.99	0.807

During the latter period, the model was less accurate in absolute terms and more accurate in relative terms. The forecasts were quite accurate in the first period because there was little variation in interest rates. However, because of limited variation, the naive model was even more accurate. While the standard error increased in the second period, the forecasting model was more accurate than the naive model in that period.

It should be pointed out that the better U value in the second period does not contradict the need for revision of the forecasting method. Evidence of bias in the model was shown in both the control chart and the prediction-realization chart; accuracy can be improved by eliminating bias.

COMPARABILITY IN USE OF
QUANTITATIVE ACCURACY MEASURES

Quantitative accuracy measures are frequently used to compare forecasters and forecasting methods. It is therefore important that these methods be used in a way that assures comparability. Several guidelines must be followed if the measures are to be genuinely comparable and useful.

First, comparison of the size of a forecasting error to variance around the mean is seldom useful. Many economic series follow an upward trend over time with some variance around that upward trend. Prediction that GNP will be higher in 1984 than its average for the last one hundred years is not a noteworthy achievement. The trick is to predict how much 1980 GNP will differ from the 1979 value. Thus, many evaluations concentrate on the ability to forecast change rather than the actual value of the series.

163

It is also important to distinguish between goodness-of-fit measures and forecast accuracy measures. The difference between the two measures is illustrated in Figure 10–3. The dots in the figure represent historical observations, and the line is drawn to fit those observations. The circled dots represent observations after the line was drawn. A standard error based on the difference between the uncircled dots and the line is a measure of historical goodness of fit. The circled dots are used in computing the forecast standard error. While both of these measures have uses, care should be taken to avoid comparing the forecasting standard error (or any variation thereof) to the standard error over the model development period. This should be attempted only if the specific purpose of the comparison is to see if the model is doing as well at forecasting as it did at explaining past observations.

In comparing the accuracy of different forecasting methods, it is important to use the same time period. A gasoline sales forecasting model tested over the period from 1963 through 1972 would likely have produced smaller average errors than a model tested over the period from 1964 through 1973 because the latter period included the first oil boycott.

In general, conditions must be made as comparable as possible if forecasters or forecasting methods are to be compared. Accuracy of forecasts prepared three months in advance cannot be strictly compared with forecasts prepared six months in advance. Forecasts of those with inside information cannot be strictly compared with those of people working without privileged information, etc.

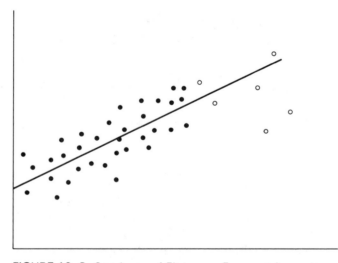

FIGURE 10–3 Goodness of Fit versus Forecast Accuracy

NONQUANTITATIVE EVALUATION OF FORECAST ACCURACY

In addition to forecasting accuracy over actual historical periods or holdout historical periods, the potential accuracy of a forecast can be evaluated by an examination of the forecasting method itself. A forecasting method should be supported by logic. Otherwise, there is the danger that what appears to be excellent forecasting ability is actually a spurious correlation over the test period. Only the logical evaluation of the forecasting model can point to such dangers.

The interest rate forecasting model used for Table 10-1 can be evaluated by comparing it to what economic theory has to say about interest rates. The forecasting model was actually based on a single variable: the ratio of nonworking people to working people. The model used this variable with a six-year lag because this lag provided the best fit. To begin with, there was no logic in support of the six-year lag; it was chosen because it gave the best fit. In addition, economic theory would suggest several other variables, including the inflation rate and Federal Reserve policy. Ignoring the inflation rate caused the large errors in this case. As the inflation rate reached higher levels, the failure to include inflation resulted in larger and larger underestimates. The evaluation of the model in comparison to economic theory may have revealed the potential for such large errors in advance of their occurrence.

Finally, the assumptions underlying the forecast should be clearly stated. GNP forecasts are inevitably based on assumptions about government taxation and spending. Interest forecasts are based on assumptions about Federal Reserve policy. Many economic forecasts are based on assumptions about OPEC policy concerning price and quantity of oil shipped. Obviously, changes in these conditions can lead to large forecasting errors. For particularly critical factors, it is helpful to perform sensitivity analysis by preparing forecasts under alternate assumptions. For example, an economic model would be run under several alternative assumptions about the quantity and price of foreign oil shipped.

SUMMARY

There are three general approaches to evaluating the accuracy of forecasting methods. The graphical approaches are used primarily as quality control methods to single out types of errors and identify developing problems with the models. The quantitative methods are used to compare forecasters or forecasting methods. Also, if certain conditions are met, quantitative methods can be used to estimate confidence intervals for forecasts. Finally, regardless of how well the forecasting model has performed in the past, the model itself and the assumptions underlying it should be considered in judging accuracy.

PROBLEMS

1. Following are actual data and forecasts prepared with the use of exponential smoothing. Prepare a control chart and a prediction-realization diagram. Should the forecasting method be revised? If so, what particular types of forecasting errors need to be addressed?

Period	Actual	Forecast	Period	Actual	Forecast
1	991		20	1083	1106
2	1003	1004	21	1067	1086
3	1014	1003	22	1082	1062
4	1019	1018	23	1093	1085
5	1034	1024	24	1098	1099
6	1038	1043	25	1114	1104
7	1054	1045	26	1099	1124
8	1038	1065	27	1113	1099
9	1027	1038	28	1122	1119
10	1018	1023	29	1134	1129
11	1014	1012	30	1139	1143
12	1022	1009	31	1148	1147
13	1034	1022	32	1159	1156
14	1039	1039	33	1174	1168
15	1053	1044	34	1183	1186
16	1062	1062	35	1188	1194
17	1068	1071	36	1202	1196
18	1079	1076	37	1187	1213
19	1094	1088	38	1179	1187
			39	1173	1176

2. For the series in problem 1, compute the mean squared error, the average error, and the U. Using these methods, comment on the accuracy of the forecasting method.

3. Do the error terms in problem 1 meet the conditions necessary for use in confidence interval estimation. If not, why? If yes, assume a forecast of 1,170 for next period and prepare a 95 percent confidence interval.

4. A particular forecasting model has resulted in a mean squared error of 82.5 and an average error of 74.3. The series of errors has been examined and meets the requirements for confidence interval estimation. The forecast for next period is 1,283. Prepare 67 percent, 95 percent, and 99 percent confidence intervals.

BASIC STATISTICAL CONCEPTS

SUMMATION (Σ)

The summation sign is a form of widely used statistical shorthand. It instructs you to sum up a series of numbers, possibly after performing some other operation on them. To understand the summation sign, it is helpful to think of numbers as being in an array. The array shown below contains eight numbers. The first number is denoted X_1, the second number is denoted X_2, etc. Thus X_1 is 112, X_2 is 120, etc.

i	1	2	3	4	5	6	7	8
X_i	112	120	130	120	110	110	140	160

The summation sign $\sum\limits_{i=3}^{5} X_i$ tells us to sum X_3 through X_5. Thus,

$$\sum_{i=3}^{5} X_i = X_3 + X_4 + X_5 = 130 + 120 + 110 = 360$$

If the intention is to sum all of the items in the array, the instruction can be simplified to $\sum\limits_{i} X_i$ or even $\sum X$. Thus $\sum X$ is interpreted as

$$X = 112 + 120 + 130 + 120 + 110 + 110 + 140 + 160 = 1,002$$

Frequently, an operation is called for, such as

$$\frac{1}{3} \sum_{i=1}^{3} (X_i - 100)^2$$

The operation on the right hand of the summation sign is completed for each value of X before summing. The operation on the left side of the summation sign is taken on the sum. Thus,

$$\frac{1}{3} \sum_{i=1}^{3} (X_i - 100)^2 = \frac{1}{3}[(112 - 100)^2 + (120 - 100)^2 + (130 - 100)^2] = 481.33$$

Exercises

i	1	2	3	4	5
Y_i	20	15	25	35	25

Use the above array to complete the following exercises:

a) $\displaystyle\sum_{i=1}^{5} Y_i$

b) $\displaystyle\sum_{i=2}^{5} Y_i^2$

c) $\displaystyle\sum \frac{1}{Y_i}$

d) $\displaystyle\sum (Y_i - 24)^2$

e) $\displaystyle\frac{1}{5} \sum Y_i$

Solutions

a) $20 + 15 + 25 + 35 + 25 = 120$

b) $15^2 + 25^2 + 35^2 + 25^2 = 2{,}700$

c) $\dfrac{1}{20} + \dfrac{1}{15} + \dfrac{1}{25} + \dfrac{1}{35} + \dfrac{1}{25} = 0.22524$

d) $(20 - 24)^2 + (15 - 24)^2 + (25 - 24)^2 + (35 - 24)^2 + (25 - 24)^2 = 220$

e) $\dfrac{1}{5}(20 + 15 + 25 + 35 + 25) = 24$

MEAN $(\overline{X})$

The mean or average of some series of values is simply the sum of the series divided by the number of values in the series (denoted n). In summation notation, this is expressed

$$\overline{X} = \frac{1}{n} \sum X$$

The following array of numbers is denoted array Z.

i	1	2	3	4	5	6
Z_i	12	15	13	18	14	12

The mean of this series is

$$\overline{Z} = \frac{1}{6} \sum Z = \frac{1}{6}(12 + 15 + 13 + 18 + 14 + 12) = 14$$

VARIANCE (σ^2)

The variance is the average squared difference between values in a series of numbers and the mean of that series. Using summation notation, the variance of a series denoted X is

$$\sigma_X^2 = \frac{1}{n} \sum (X - \overline{X})^2$$

For the array denoted as Z above, the mean ($\overline{Z}$) was computed as 14. The variance of the series is then

$$\sigma_Z^2 = \frac{1}{6} \sum (Z - \overline{Z})^2 = \frac{1}{6} [(12 - 14)^2 + (15 - 14)^2 + (13 - 14)^2 +$$
$$(18 - 14)^2 + (14 - 14)^2 + (12 - 14)^2] = 4.333$$

The *standard deviation* is denoted as σ and is the square root of the variance. Thus, the standard deviation for the above series is

$$\sigma_Z = \sqrt{4.333} = 2.08$$

The variance and standard deviation serve as measures of the dispersion of a series around its mean. These measures will prove particularly useful when discussing the accuracy of forecasting methods.

COVARIANCE (σ_{XY})

The covariance measures the tendency of two variables to move or vary together. The covariance of a series is defined as

$$\sigma_{XY} = \frac{1}{n} \sum (X - \overline{X})(Y - \overline{Y})$$

Below are two series, one denoted Q and one denoted R

i	1	2	3	4	5
Q_i	10	8	12	15	10
R_i	4	2	5	5	4

For these series,

$$\overline{Q} = \frac{1}{5} (10 + 8 + 12 + 15 + 10) = 11$$

$$\overline{R} = \frac{1}{5} (4 + 2 + 5 + 5 + 4) = 4$$

$$\sigma_{QR} = \frac{1}{5}[(10 - 11)(4 - 4) + (8 - 11)(2 - 4) + (12 - 11)(5 - 4)$$
$$+ (15 - 11)(5 - 4) + (10 - 11)(4 - 4)] = 2.2$$

The covariance above is positive, indicating that when Q is above its mean, R is also likely to be above its mean, and vice versa. If the covariance is negative, the two series are related in that they tend to move in opposite directions.

COMPUTATIONAL AIDS

The formulas given above are helpful for understanding the mean, variance and covariance, but there are easier computation formulas available. These are

$$\sigma_X^2 = \frac{1}{n}\sum X^2 - \overline{X}^2$$

$$\sigma_{XY} = \frac{1}{n}\sum XY - \overline{XY}$$

Using these two formulas for the series denoted Q and R above,

$$\sigma_Q^2 = \frac{1}{5}(10^2 + 8^2 + 12^2 + 15^2 + 10^2) - 11^2 = 5.6$$

$$\sigma_{QR} = \frac{1}{5}(10 \cdot 4 + 8 \cdot 2 + 12 \cdot 5 + 15 \cdot 5 + 10 \cdot 4) - 4 \cdot 11 = 2.2$$

Exercise

For the series of numbers below, compute the mean, variance, standard deviation, and covariance.

i	1	2	3	4
X_i	110	80	90	120
Y_i	7	4	5	8

Answers

$$\overline{X} = 100 \qquad \sigma_X^2 = 250 \qquad \sigma_X = 15.8$$

$$\overline{Y} = 6 \qquad \sigma_Y^2 = 2.5 \qquad \sigma_Y = 1.58$$

$$\sigma_{XY} = 25$$

NORMAL DISTRIBUTION

Many characteristics studied by forecasters have distributions that are approximately normal: the bell-shaped, symmetrical form illustrated in Figure A-1. The horizontal axis represents some characteristic, such as weight. The point $\overline{X}$ represents the mean value while other points on the horizontal axis represent deviations from the mean, measured in numbers of standard deviations. Thus, if the mean weight of a particular population is 150 pounds and the standard deviation is 10 pounds, the point +1.96 on the horizontal axis represents 169.6 pounds ($150 + 1.96 \cdot 10$). The proportion of the shaded area in Figure A-1 to the total area under the curve represents the proportion of the population with weights between 150 and 169.6 pounds. Appendix D contains the proportion of the area under the curve with a value between the mean and a number of different standard deviations above the mean.

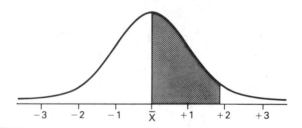

FIGURE A-1 The Normal Distribution

Using the above weight example, the probability of a weight between 150 and 169.6 pounds ($\overline{X} + 1.96$ standard deviations) is found from Appendix D to be .4750. Since the distribution is symmetrical, the probability of a weight between 130.4 and 169.6 ($\overline{X} \pm 1.96$ standard deviations) is .9500 ($.4750 \cdot 2$). Since there is a .5 probability of a value above the mean, the probability of a randomly drawn individual weighing more than 169.6 is .0250 ($.5000 - .4750$).

COMMONLY USED DATA SOURCES*

GUIDES TO DATA

Business Serials of the U.S. Government. American Library Association. Chicago, Ill.

This publication consists of an annotated list of serials covering business and financial activity.

American Statistics Index. Congressional Information Service. Washington D.C.

This publication provides a guide to the various sources of government statistics. For example, a forecaster interested in corn production would find listed eight different U.S. government publications in which corn production and price statistics appear.

CIS/Index to Publications of the United States Government. Congressional Information Service. Washington, D.C.

This publication represents the most complete and timely listing of publications of the U.S. Congress. These include documents, laws, reports, and hearing records. Of course, large quantities of economic data are included.

*Arranged by frequency of use within topics.

Yakes, Nancy and Denise Akey, eds. *Encyclopedia of Associations.* Gale Research Company. Detroit, Michigan. Annual

This guide provides the names and addresses of nearly all associations in the United States. It can be used to identify an association that might compile data needed by the forecaster.

Predicasts and *Worldcasts,* Predicasts, Inc. Cleveland, Ohio.

In addition to their own forecasts, these publications provide summaries and bibliographies of forecasts prepared by others. For example, *Predicasts* could be used to prepare a bibliography of shoe sales forecasts for the United States. Each quarterly edition contains several pages of fine print references to GNP forecasts.

Encyclopedia of Information Systems and Services, 4th ed. Gale Research Company. Detroit, Michigan. 1981.

This volume, with its periodic updates, provides a listing of data services with a brief description of the type of data available from each service. It contains sources of international information, such as a computerized economic data base for Hong Kong, as well as sources in the United States. This encyclopedia is particularly useful for locating computerized data bases.

Business Periodicals Index. The H. Wilson Co. New York.

This is the basic reference source used for locating articles on the various aspects of business and economics. Of course, very few of the articles represent basic data sources. They do, however, represent sources of forecasts, forecasting methods, and references to relevant basic data sources.

SOURCES OF GENERAL DATA

Statistical Abstract of the United States. U.S. Bureau of the Census. Washington D.C. Annual.

This publication is a compilation of statistics on many aspects of American life, including economic activity, demographic characteristics, health, education, transportation, crime, etc. It also provides many useful references to other sources. If the forecaster were to purchase only one volume of data, this would be it.

Historical Statistics of the United States. U.S. Bureau of the Census. Washington, D.C.

This publication contains historical values for many of the series in the *Statistical Abstract* dating as far back as the Colonial period.

Economic Report of the President. United States Government Printing Office. Washington, D.C. Annual.

This volume is submitted to Congress each year in keeping with the provisions of the Full Employment Act of 1946. A major part of the publication is a statistical appendix concerning the labor force, inflation, economic activity, and economic well-being of the population. Thus it is a useful source of many series used in business forecasting.

SOURCES OF GENERAL ECONOMIC DATA

Survey of Current Business. Bureau of Economic Analysis, U.S. Department of Commerce. Washington, D.C.

This publication is the primary compilation with regard to Gross National Product and its components. Data is broken down to detail levels such that the *Survey* can be used to study historical patterns of specific items such as hide shipments or copper prices. The biannual supplements provide historical compilations for various series. Most serious forecasters subscribe to the *Survey.*

Business Conditions Digest. Bureau of Economic Analysis, U.S. Department of Commerce. Washington, D.C. Monthly.

This monthly chartbook of economic series is the primary source of data on leading economic indicators. It is used for short-term forecasting of economic activity.

Statistical Bulletin. The Conference Board, Inc. New York. Monthly.

In addition to some other data, this publication contains the most recent GNP forecasts from several econometric models and a survey of working forecasters.

Readings in Concepts and Methods of National Income Statistics. National Technical Information Service. Washington, D.C.

This volume provides a valuable source of background information on the definitions, sources of data, and statistical calculations used in preparing the national income and product accounts.

Dictionary of Economic and Statistical Terms. U.S. Department of Commerce. Washington, D.C.

This is a helpful source of information on the meanings of economic data.

SOURCES OF DATA ON GOVERNMENT
ACTIVITY

Social Security Bulletin. Social Security Administration, U.S. Department of Health, Education, and Welfare. Washington, D.C. Monthly.

The bulletin reports current data on the operations of the Social Security Administration and the results of research and analysis pertinent to the Social Security program.

Quarterly Summary of State and Local Tax Revenues. U.S. Bureau of the Census, U.S. Department of Commerce. Washington, D.C.

This publication reports state and local taxes collected by type and state. Some data is also given for selected cities.

The Budget of the United States Government. Office of Management and Budget, Executive Office of the President. Washington, D.C. Annual.

The budget, submitted by the president each January, contains planned federal expenditures for the upcoming year. The *Appendix* and *Special Analysis* are volumes that provide more detail than that found in the six hundred pages of the main budget document. *The United States Budget in Brief* provides an eighty-five page summary for those needing less detail than appears in the budget itself.

Federal Reserve Bulletin. Board of Governors of the Federal Reserve System. Washington, D.C. Monthly.

This publication contains statistical series on banks and financial markets as well as incidental material on inflation and economic activity. It is on the subscription lists of most serious forecasters.

Standard and Poor's Statistical Service. Standard and Poor's Corporation. New York. Annual.

This service is published as an annual volume with monthly updates. It contains monthly data and even weekly data on financial markets going back to the nineteenth century. It also contains inflation data and economic activity data by industry category.

Statistical Bulletin. Securities and Exchange Commission. Washington, D.C.

These publications include data on gross proceeds from all new securities issues. Information on issues by industry and type is also provided, as is information on the cost of issues. In addition, information about exchange volume and prices is included.

178

Treasury Bulletin. Department of the Treasury. Washington, D.C.

> This monthly publication contains information on volume, maturity, and ownership of government debt. It is particularly useful for those interested in the impact of government debt operations on financial markets.

Conference Board Quarterly Survey of Capital Appropriations. The Conference Board, Inc. New York.

> Based on a survey of capital expenditure and appropriations, this publication provides a complete breakdown of past capital expenditures and a forecast of capital expenditures for two years.

Value Line Investment Survey. Arnold Berhard and Company. New York.

> Like a number of competing services, Value Line is aimed primarily at the investment community. It contains historical data and limited forecasts of individual company performance. It includes a statement of Value Line's view of long-term (five-year) economic outlook. Some parts of the service are released as often as weekly.

Moody's Industrial Manual, Moody's Transportation Manual, Moody's Public Utility Manual, and *Moody's Bank and Finance Manual.* Moody's Investors Service, Inc. New York. Annual.

> These volumes provide a ready source of information on individual companies, primarily in the form of financial statement data.

SOURCES OF INTERNATIONAL DATA

Statistical Yearbook. Department of International Economics and Social Affairs, United Nations. New York.

> If the United Nations has not brought unity, it has at least brought unified statistics. The *Yearbook* is the beginning source for using the statistics on economic and population characteristics of the various countries. Topics include production, population, transportation, finance, health, education, and culture.

Monthly Bulletin of Statistics. Department of International Economics and Social Affairs, United Nations. New York.

> The monthly bulletins contain the most recent economic and population statistics for the various countries.

U.S. Commodity Exports and *U.S. Commodity Imports.* U.S. Bureau of the Census, U.S. Department of Commerce. Washington, D.C. Annual.

These volumes report on exports and imports by S.I.C. (Standard Industrial Classification Code). For example, these publications could be used to determine the dollar value of antacids shipped to Japan. More limited balance of payments data is also contained in the *Survey of Current Business* and the *Federal Reserve Bulletin.*

International Financial Statistics. International Monetary Fund.

This monthly publication contains detailed financial statistics as well as other economic data for countries in total and individual countries. It is a good reference for information such as the inflation rate and oil production in Bahrain for the most recent month.

SOURCES OF DATA ON MISCELLANEOUS TOPICS

County and City Data Book. U.S. Bureau of the Census, Department of Commerce. Washington. D.C.

This supplement to the *Statistical Abstract of the United States* is published every four years. It contains economic and population data broken down by city and county.

Employment and Earnings. U.S. Department of Labor. Washington, D.C. Monthly.

Just as the *Survey of Current Business* is the primary source of Gross National Product related data, this monthly publication is the primary source of labor force and unemployment data. Data is broken down by industry, area, and demographic characteristic.

Handbook of Labor Statistics. U.S. Department of Labor. Washington, D.C. Annual.

This volume contains historical data for many of the series in *Employment and Earnings.*

The Census of Business

The Census of Manufacturing

The Census of Mining

The Census of Agriculture

The Census of Transportation
> U.S. Bureau of the Census, Department of Commerce. Washington, D.C.

> This group of censuses provides detailed information for many groups of industries. Geographic breakdowns by industry are also included. While most of the titles are self-explanatory, the *Census of Business* covers only retailing.

Current Population Reports. U.S. Bureau of the Census, Department of Commerce. Washington, D.C.

> There are actually several different series under this general heading. They include *Population Characteristics, Special Studies, Farm Population, Consumer Income, Population Estimates and Projections,* and *Special Censuses.* These series contain the most recent estimates and projections compiled by the Bureau of the Census on the various topics mentioned. For example, *Consumer Income* is a thrice yearly volume covering the proportions of families and persons at various income levels as well as data on the relationship of income to age, sex, color, family size, education, occupation, work experience, and other characteristics. *Population Estimates and Projections* contains current data on many aspects of the population as well as projections.

Statistics of Income. Internal Revenue Service. Washington, D.C.

> This series of publications contains information on categories of income and expenses for the various groups listed. Data is broken down by state and region. Publications within the series include:
> Business Income Tax Returns
> Sole Proprietorships and Partnerships
> Corporate Income Tax Returns
> Individual Income Tax Returns
> Personal Wealth Estimated from Estate Tax Returns.

Consumer Attitudes and Buying Plans. The Conference Board, Inc. New York. Monthly.

> This series reports on the current results of surveys of consumer confidence and buying plans.

COMPUTER-BASED DATA SERVICES

Compuserve, Inc.
> 5000 Arlington Centre Blvd., Columbus, Ohio 43220

> Compuserve is the largest provider of computerized data services. It serves personal computer users through its Personal Computing Division. It provides time-sharing computer services and electronic mail services as well as various data bases. In addition to other data, the service provides a broad range of stock market information.

181

The Source

1616 Anderson Rd., McLean, Va. 22102

This is another of the services that provide access to a number of major data bases through a personal computer. It also provides computer programs, electronic mail, and other computer communication services. In addition to other information, the service provides a broad range of stock market information.

Standard and Poor's Stockpack

This is one of several services that specialize in providing information that is primarily of interest to investors. The information can be used to analyze and forecast investment performance.

TABLE OF THE *t* STATISTIC

Two Tails	$p = .20$	$p = .10$	$p = .05$	$p = .02$	$p = .01$	Degrees of Freedom
One Tail	$p = .10$	$p = .05$	$p = .020$	$p = .01$	$p = .005$	
1	3.078	6.314	12.706	31.821	63.657	1
2	1.886	2.920	4.303	6.965	9.925	2
3	1.638	2.353	3.182	4.541	5.841	3
4	1.533	2.132	2.776	3.747	4.604	4
5	1.476	2.015	2.571	3.365	4.032	5
6	1.440	1.943	2.447	3.143	3.707	6
7	1.415	1.895	2.365	2.998	3.499	7
8	1.397	1.860	2.306	2.896	3.355	8
9	1.383	1.833	2.262	2.821	3.250	9
10	1.372	1.812	2.228	2.764	3.169	10
11	1.363	1.796	2.201	2.718	3.106	11
12	1.356	1.782	2.179	2.681	3.055	12
13	1.350	1.771	2.160	2.650	3.012	13
14	1.345	1.761	2.145	2.624	2.977	14
15	1.341	1.753	2.131	2.602	2.947	15
16	1.337	1.746	2.120	2.583	2.921	16
17	1.333	1.740	2.110	2.567	2.898	17
18	1.330	1.734	2.101	2.552	2.878	18

Table of the t Statistic

Two Tails	$p = .20$	$p = .10$	$p = .05$	$p = .02$	$p = .01$	Degrees of
One Tail	$p = .10$	$p = .05$	$p = .020$	$p = .01$	$p = .005$	Freedom
19	1.328	1.729	2.093	2.539	2.861	19
20	1.325	1.725	2.086	2.528	2.845	20
21	1.323	1.721	2.080	2.518	2.831	21
22	1.321	1.717	2.074	2.508	2.819	22
23	1.319	1.714	2.069	2.500	2.807	23
24	1.318	1.711	2.064	2.492	2.797	24
25	1.316	1.708	2.060	2.485	2.787	25
26	1.315	1.706	2.056	2.479	2.779	26
27	1.314	1.703	2.052	2.473	2.771	27
28	1.313	1.701	2.048	2.467	2.763	28
29	1.311	1.699	2.045	2.462	2.756	29
inf.	1.282	1.645	1.960	2.326	2.576	inf.

Based on Table 12 of *Biometrika Tables for Statisticians*, Vol. I, Third Edition (1966), Cambridge University Press. Used by permission of the *Biometrika* Trustees.

THE STANDARD NORMAL DISTRIBUTION

z	.00	.01	.02	.03	.04	.05	.06	.07	.08	.09
0.0	.0000	.0040	.0080	.0120	.0160	.0199	.0239	.0279	.0319	.0359
0.1	.0398	.0438	.0478	.0517	.0557	.0596	.0636	.0675	.0714	.0753
0.2	.0793	.0832	.0871	.0910	.0948	.0987	.1026	.1064	.1103	.1141
0.3	.1179	.1217	.1255	.1293	.1331	.1368	.1406	.1443	.1480	.1517
0.4	.1554	.1591	.1628	.1664	.1700	.1736	.1772	.1808	.1844	.1879
0.5	.1915	.1950	.1985	.2019	.2054	.2088	.2123	.2157	.2190	.2224
0.6	.2257	.2291	.2324	.2357	.2389	.2422	.2454	.2486	.2517	.2549
0.7	.2580	.2611	.2642	.2673	.2704	.2734	.2764	.2794	.2823	.2852
0.8	.2881	.2910	.2939	.2967	.2995	.3023	.3051	.3078	.3106	.3133
0.9	.3159	.3186	.3212	.3238	.3264	.3289	.3315	.3340	.3365	.3389
1.0	.3413	.3438	.3461	.3485	.3508	.3531	.3554	.3577	.3599	.3621
1.1	.3643	.3665	.3686	.3708	.3729	.3749	.3770	.3790	.3810	.3830
1.2	.3849	.3869	.3888	.3907	.3925	.3944	.3962	.3980	.3997	.4015
1.3	.4032	.4049	.4066	.4082	.4099	.4115	.4131	.4147	.4162	.4177
1.4	.4192	.4207	.4222	.4236	.4251	.4265	.4279	.4292	.4306	.4319
1.5	.4332	.4345	.4357	.4370	.4382	.4394	.4406	.4418	.4429	.4441
1.6	.4452	.4463	.4474	.4484	.4495	.4505	.4515	.4525	.4535	.4545
1.7	.4554	.4564	.4573	.4582	.4591	.4599	.4608	.4616	.4625	.4633
1.8	.4641	.4649	.4656	.4664	.4671	.4678	.4686	.4693	.4699	.4706
1.9	.4713	.4719	.4726	.4732	.4738	.4744	.4750	.4756	.4761	.4767

z	.00	.01	.02	.03	.04	.05	.06	.07	.08	.09
2.0	.4772	.4778	.4783	.4788	.4793	.4798	.4803	.4808	.4812	.4817
2.1	.4821	.4826	.4830	.4834	.4838	.4842	.4846	.4850	.4854	.4857
2.2	.4861	.4864	.4868	.4871	.4875	.4878	.4881	.4884	.4887	.4890
2.3	.4893	.4896	.4898	.4901	.4904	.4906	.4909	.4911	.4913	.4916
2.4	.4918	.4920	.4922	.4925	.4927	.4929	.4931	.4932	.4934	.4936
2.5	.4938	.4940	.4941	.4943	.4945	.4946	.4948	.4949	.4951	.4952
2.6	.4953	.4955	.4956	.4957	.4959	.4960	.4961	.4962	.4963	.4964
2.7	.4965	.4966	.4967	.4968	.4969	.4970	.4971	.4972	.4973	.4974
2.8	.4974	.4975	.4976	.4977	.4977	.4978	.4979	.4979	.4980	.4981
2.9	.4981	.4982	.4982	.4983	.4984	.4984	.4985	.4985	.4986	.4986
3.0	.4987	.4987	.4987	.4988	.4988	.4989	.4989	.4989	.4990	.4990

INDEX